Healing the Wound
of Humanity

Healing the Wound of Humanity

*The Spirituality of
John Henry Newman*

Ian Ker

DARTON·LONGMAN+TODD

First published in 1993 by
Darton, Longman and Todd Ltd
1 Spencer Court
140–142 Wandsworth High Street
London SW18 4JJ

ISBN 0–232–52034–8

A catalogue record for this book is available
from the British Library

Phototypeset by Intype, London
Printed and bound in Great Britain
at the University Press, Cambridge

CONTENTS

ACKNOWLEDGEMENTS

This book has grown out of some talks I gave at a retreat in Lent 1992 for members of 'Cor ad Cor'. I dedicate it to them and to all who belong to this fledgling lay movement inspired by John Henry Newman.

I owe several improvements in the text to my friend the Revd Dr James Reidy of the University of St Thomas, Minnesota, USA.

1

THE PERSONAL NATURE OF RELIGIOUS BELIEF

Newman spent a good deal of his life trying to show that the tenaciously held beliefs of everyday life are not irrational but highly reasonable, even if they do not fall within the compass of empirical or logical demonstration. After all, if we were only prepared to say that we felt assured of being right in the latter kind of cases, then life would be not only rather barren of assurance, but we would have to say that we were uncertain about those very things which are personally most important to us – like a man's assurance that his wife loves him. Of course Newman knew perfectly well that beliefs may turn out to be mistaken; but then it is also possible to make mistakes even in matters of objectively verifiable knowledge.

The personal element in our beliefs varies according to the subject-matter. We are no longer talking about proofs as in demonstrable matters of knowledge, but really about judgment, or what Newman came to call the *illative sense.* Clearly the husband considering the question of his wife's fidelity, the detective trying to solve a crime, and the art historian investigating the authenticity of a picture, are individually not only looking at very different kinds of evidence but also employing their own distinctive types of judgment. In the case of the art historian the moral element is not relevant at all, whereas for the detective estimates of the truthfulness of witnesses are highly material, and for the husband his evaluation of his wife's character is by far and away the most important part of the judgment he has to make.

Newman thought that in religious belief too it is the personal moral element which is the most decisive factor. Othello came to hold his tragically wrong belief about Desdemona's fidelity because (arguably) of the flaw of jealousy in his own character which so grossly clouded his judgment. Newman held that the religious believer is someone whose judgment is in good working order because he or she has the right moral dispositions, whereas the unbeliever's judgment is morally flawed, whether voluntarily or involuntarily.

Religious belief, therefore, is as personal a matter, as each of us has only our own personal conscience to use in making moral decisions since we cannot use anyone else's conscience. To say, then, that religious belief is a subjective matter is not at all to say that it is irrational or unreasonable but it is to recognize that it involves personal judgment which in turn involves our moral principles. This is why Newman could tell his younger brother Charles, when as young men they were arguing about religion, that 'the rejection of Christianity' rises 'from a fault of the heart, not of the intellect', since a 'dislike of the contents of Scripture is at the bottom of unbelief'. Hence it is that 'the most powerful arguments for Christianity do not *convince*, only *silence*; for there is at the bottom that secret antipathy for the doctrines of Christianity, which is quite out of the reach of argument'. Already for Newman the key question is not so much What are the arguments in favour of belief? as What are the personal factors that in fact move a particular person to believe or not to believe? And crucial here is the importance of what Newman was later to call 'antecedent probability', a point he had already grasped in his early twenties when he wrote:

> We survey moral and religious subjects through the glass of previous habits; and scarcely two persons use a glass of the same magnifying power. I venture confidently to say, that if the contents of a professed revelation on divine things are to be made the test of its genuineness, *no revelation could* be made us; for scarcely two persons can be got together, who will agree in

their antecedent or self-originated ideas of God and his purposes towards man.[1]

In other words, our religious beliefs (or lack of) depend on what we think is likely to be true, and this in turn depends on the kind of people we are, and what our values are. All our beliefs and convictions stem from whatever 'first principles' (as Newman calls them) we hold in the relevant case. All our views rest on certain premises or presuppositions, so that:

> First Principles . . . are the means of proof, and are not themselves proved; they are sovereign on the one hand, irresponsible on the other: they are absolute monarchs . . . they are to the mind what the circulation of the blood and the various functions of our animal organs are to the body . . . they are, in short, the man.[2]

Like all our beliefs, religious belief is 'influenced . . . less by evidence, more by previously-entertained principles, views, and wishes', that is, by 'antecedent probabilities', and it is when these 'prepossessions' are right, that 'we are right in believing', albeit 'upon slender evidence'. What distinguishes religious belief from other kinds of belief is that the 'probabilities' which create it depend on one's 'moral temperament', for 'A good man and a bad man will think very different things probable'. Unlike many other of our beliefs, religious belief involves moral responsibility: 'a man *is* responsible for his faith, because he is responsible for his likings and dislikings, his hopes and his opinions, on all of which his faith depends'. These 'feelings', which are deeply personal although they 'come only of supernatural grace', are what 'make us think evidence sufficient, which falls short of a proof in itself'. And so, Newman claims, 'religious minds embrace the Gospel mainly on the great antecedent probability of a Revelation, and the suitableness of the Gospel to their needs'. On the other hand, the formal arguments for Christianity are not only 'thrown away' on 'men of irreligious minds', but too much stress on 'arguments from facts' encourages people 'to think that Faith is mainly

the result of argument' and that 'religious Truth is a legitimate matter of disputation' without any 'preparation of
heart'. This does not make Newman a fideist: he does not
hold the 'wild' anti-intellectual 'notion that actually no proof
at all is implied in the maintenance, or may be exacted for
the profession of Christianity'. His view is simply that 'it is
antecedent probability that gives meaning to those arguments from facts which are commonly called the Evidences
of Religion; and that, whereas mere probability proves
nothing, mere facts persuade no one; that probability is to
fact, as the soul to the body'.[3]

What, however, is probable to one person will not seem
probable to another person. For an 'active', 'personal and
living' faith is created by 'anticipations and presumptions'
that 'are the creation of the mind itself', while the 'external
religion' this involves 'elicits into shape, and supplies the
spontaneous desires and presentiments of their minds'. The
arguments for Christianity cannot compel faith: a person
believes on the personal testimony of 'the state of his heart'.
But the arguments anyway look differently to different
people: 'the antecedent judgement, with which a man
approaches the subject of religion, not only acts as a bearing
this way or that, – as causing him to go out to meet the
evidence in a greater or less degree, and nothing more, –
but, further, it practically colours the evidence'. Unbelief is
as personal a matter as belief, since it for its part 'criticizes
the evidence of Religion, only because it does not like it,
and really goes upon presumptions and prejudices as much
as Faith does, only presumptions of an opposite nature'. The
conclusion Newman reaches in his Anglican *Oxford University
Sermons* (1843) is that 'We *believe*, because we *love*'. It is the
'divinely-enlightened mind' which 'sees in Christ the very
Object whom it desires to love and worship, – the Object
correlative of its own affections'. And so while Newman
insists on the intellectual element of reasoning in religious
belief, he also emphasizes the personal nature of the act of
faith, which 'is a reasoning upon holy, devout, and enlightened presumptions', 'takes its character from the moral

state of the agent', and 'is perfected, not by intellectual cultivation, but by obedience'.[4]

The problem with the argument from probability was, Newman came to feel, that it tended to undermine the idea of certainty. And so he tried to 'complete' his theory of belief by arguing that 'absolute certitude . . . was the result of an *assemblage* of concurring and converging probabilities' and that 'probabilities which did not reach to logical certainty, might suffice for a mental certitude; that the certitude thus brought about might equal in measure and strength the certitude which was created by the strictest scientific demonstration'.[5] Thus a 'collection of weak evidences' can together make up 'a strong evidence', so that there is 'a converging evidence' which 'amounts to proof'. But for deciding whether there is enough probability for conviction, one has to use one's own personal 'prudent judgment'.[6] And so 'the measure of probability necessary for certainty' will vary 'with the individual mind'.[7]

After his conversion to the Roman Catholic Church, Newman became even more alive to the danger of appearing to suggest that belief is irrational. But he continued to argue that a reasonable faith was 'the result of converging probabilities, and a cumulative proof' from 'cumulating probabilities'.[8] Because in this kind of non-logical, non-scientific reasoning, the 'cumulation of probabilities, over and above their implicit character, will vary both in their number and their separate estimated value, according to the particular intellect which is employed upon it', it 'follows that what to one intellect is a proof is not so to another, and that the certainty of a proposition does properly consist in the certitude of the mind which contemplates it'.[9] In spite of the danger, then, of giving the impression that religious belief is merely subjective in a pejorative sense, Newman did not abandon his view of the ultimately personal nature of religious belief. To say that this kind of reasoning is personal is not to say that it is subjective. There is nothing, for instance, subjective in a pejorative sense in believing that one day I shall die, although this is a conviction of mine that is neither empirically demonstrable (since it is an event lying in the future) nor susceptible to logical proof:

> But what logic cannot do, my own living personal reasoning, my good sense, which is the healthy condition of such personal reasoning, but which cannot adequately express itself in words, does for me, and I am possessed with the most precise, absolute, masterful certitude of my dying some day or other.

The fact is, says Newman, that not only our religious beliefs but also 'many of our most obstinate and most reasonable certitudes depend on proofs which are informal and personal, which baffle our powers of analysis, and cannot be brought under logical rule, because they cannot be submitted to logical statistics'.

It is not surprising, then, that 'an intellectual question may strike two minds very differently, may awaken in them distinct associations, may be invested by them in contrary characteristics, and lead them to opposite conclusions'. For in what Newman calls 'concrete reasonings', we 'judge for ourselves, by our own lights, and on our own principles; and our criterion of truth is not so much the manipulation of propositions, as the intellectual and moral character of the person maintaining them'. In other words, because a person's beliefs are personal, ultimately they will depend on what kind of a person he or she is. This does not mean that all beliefs are merely relative and subjective, it is rather the case

> that truth there is, and attainable it is, but that its rays stream in upon us through the medium of our moral as well as our intellectual being; and that in consequence that perception of its first principles which is natural to us is enfeebled, obstructed, perverted, by allurements of sense and the supremacy of self, and, on the other hand, quickened by aspirations after the supernatural; so that at length two characters of mind are brought out into shape, and two standards and systems of thought, – each logical, when analyzed, yet

contradictory of each other, and only not antagonistic because they have no common ground on which they can conflict.[10]

Because the first principles that are most relevant to religious belief are moral ones, a good person is more likely to be a believer than a bad person. For to 'attempt to *see*' these first principles 'by means of the intellect' rather than by the conscience was, Newman thought, similar to the mistake of 'attempting by the intellect to see the physical facts' which are perceived by the senses, which in turn '*enable* the intellect to act, by giving it something to act upon'.[11] The modern insistence on simply using the intellect in religious inquiry was, he believed, analogous to the medieval Schoolmen's use of syllogistic reasoning instead of empirical observation in scientific investigation. In fact, of course, Newman thought that the unbeliever refuses to believe not on so-called rational grounds but ultimately because of different first principles which lead as inexorably to unbelief as the moral first principles of the believer lead to faith.

In faith, then, and in all the important beliefs in life that we cannot prove, Newman holds that 'that supra-logical judgment, which is the warrant for our certitude about them, is not mere common-sense, but the true healthy action of our ratiocinative powers, an action more subtle and more comprehensive than the mere appreciation of a syllogistic argument'. This is why 'a proof, except in abstract demonstration, has always in it, more or less, an element of the personal, because "prudence" is not a constituent part of our nature, but a personal endowment'. We become certain 'by the action of our own minds, by our own individual perception of the truth in question, under a sense of duty to those conclusions and with an intellectual conscientiousness'. In this kind of non-logical thinking, where personality is such an important factor,

> the conclusion . . . is foreseen and predicted rather than actually attained; foreseen in the number and direction of accumulated premisses, which all converge to it, and as the result of their combination, approach it more

nearly than any assignable difference, yet do not touch
it logically (though only not touching it,) on account
of the nature of its subject-matter, and the delicate and
implicit character of at least part of the reasonings on
which it depends.

And so 'it is that the practised and experienced mind is able
to make a sure divination that a conclusion is inevitable, of
which his lines of reasoning do not actually put him in
possession'.[12]

It is not, therefore, 'skill in argumentation' as much as
'judgment' which is the key to attaining to truth in non-
logical subjects. And this intellectual judgment, when it is
functioning properly, Newman calls the 'illative sense'.
Where logical proof is not available, there is no other 'warrant' we can appeal to in order to justify our being certain
apart from that 'sole and final judgment' which 'is committed to the personal action of the ratiocinative faculty, the
perfection of which I have called the Illative Sense'. While
rejecting scepticism, Newman readily admits that he can see
'no ultimate test of truth besides the testimony born to truth
by the mind itself'. The judgment of one's own mind, that
is, the illative sense, has to decide 'the limit of converging
probabilities and the reasons sufficient for a proof'. The
illative sense is also concerned with first principles, 'which
in all reasoning are assumptions . . . very often of a personal
character, which are half the battle in the inference with
which the reasoning is to terminate'. These include 'the
aspects in which a question is to be viewed', 'the principles
on which it is to be considered' and 'the arguments by which
it is decided'.[13]

While accepting that there are 'grounds intrinsically and
objectively and abstractedly demonstrative' to prove Christianity, Newman argues that such arguments are not necessarily irresistible, as is shown by the fact that people are not
in practice persuaded by them. For it is impossible to 'con-
vert' people without their sharing certain 'assumptions',
since 'without assumptions no one can prove anything about
anything'. Because, therefore, 'scientific demonstrations' are

not the way people come to faith, he asserts that 'it is more congenial to my own judgment to attempt to prove Christianity in the same informal way in which I can prove for certain that I have been born into this world, and that I shall die out of it'. But again, 'if any one starts from any other principles but ours, I have not the power to change his principles, or the conclusion which he draws from them, any more than I can make a crooked man straight'. A person may not be responsible for being 'mentally crooked', but that person will not be convinced of the truth of Christianity.[14]

2

A PERSONAL GOD

In a recent study of the arguments from human experience for the existence of God, Newman has been criticized by Aidan Nichols, OP 'for concentrating his energies so exclusively on one aspect of our experience, our awareness of moral obligation', for 'a unilateral concentration on moral experience', that is, 'our experience of conscience'.[1]

Presumably there could be no objection to Newman placing the major emphasis on conscience since in doing so he would only be reflecting the whole thrust of the Bible and the Christian tradition, summed up in the words of St Paul on the law of God that is engraved on the hearts of human beings enlightened by conscience if not by revelation.[2] But how far is it true that Newman confines himself to the moral argument for God's existence?

It is certainly true that in the *Essay in Aid of a Grammar of Assent* (1870) he calls conscience the 'great' – though not the sole – 'internal teacher of religion'. It is the great teacher since it 'is a personal guide, and I use it because I must use myself', and since it 'is nearer to me than any other means of knowledge'. In other words, what is so important about conscience is that it is both personal to the individual and a form of knowledge that is accessible to others through their consciences. As, then, conscience is both experiential and cognitive, it has a special philosophical importance for effective apologetics. And Newman says that if he had to 'prove the Being of a God', this is where he would 'look for the proof of it'. He argues that just as we become aware of the physical world through our senses:

so from the perceptive power which identifies the intimations of conscience with the reverberations or echoes
(so to say) of an external admonition, we proceed on
to the notion of a Supreme Ruler and Judge, and then
again we image Him and His attributes in those recur-
ring intimations, out of which, as mental phenomena,
our recognition of His existence was originally gained.

Giving to conscience its ordinary and primary meaning of
'a sense of duty' or a 'magisterial dictate', rather than
merely 'a moral sense', Newman explains that

conscience does not repose on itself, but vaguely
reaches forward to something beyond self, and dimly
discerns a sanction higher than self for its decisions . . .
And hence it is that we are accustomed to speak of
conscience as a voice . . . and moreover a voice, or the
echo of a voice, imperative and constraining, like no
other dictate in the whole of our experience.

Conscience, Newman continues:

always involves the recognition of a living object,
towards which it is directed. Inanimate things cannot
stir our affections; these are correlative with persons. If,
as is the case, we feel responsibility, are ashamed, are
frightened, at transgressing the voice of conscience, this
implies that there is One to whom we are responsible,
before whom we are ashamed, whose claims upon us
we fear . . . If the cause of those emotions does not
belong to this visible world, the Object to which [our]
perception is directed must be Supernatural and Divine;
and thus the phenomena of Conscience, as a dictate,
avail to impress the imagination with the picture of a
Supreme Governor, a Judge, holy, just, powerful, all-
seeing, retributive, and is the creative principle of
religion, as the Moral Sense is the principle of ethics.[3]

It has been remarked that Newman does not here 'argue
to a law of binding force and from thence, in the old
style, to a lawgiver'.[4] He himself denied that he was trying

to employ an 'abstract argument from the force of the terms', such as that 'a Law implies a Lawgiver', but that he was responding to 'the peculiarity of that feeling to which I *give* the name of Conscience'.[5] His earlier writings, however, do give some credence to the idea, as when he preaches that 'a law implies a lawgiver, and a command implies a superior'. But this quotation from a fairly early sermon (1834) is followed by the words, 'Thus a man is at once thrown out of himself, by the very Voice which speaks within him.'[6] By the time Newman came to write his novel *Callista* (1856), the argument has become completely personalized:

> '. . . it is the echo of a person speaking to me. Nothing shall persuade me that it does not ultimately proceed from a person external to me. It carries with it its proof of its divine origin. My nature feels towards it as towards a person . . . An echo implies a voice; a voice a speaker. That speaker I love and I fear.'[7]

Conscience frees a person from the narrowness of self by opening up interpersonal communion with the person of God: 'its very existence throws us out of ourselves, and beyond ourselves, to go and seek for Him in the height and depth, whose Voice it is.'[8]

In the last great chapter of the *Apologia* (1864), where Newman offers a general defence of Roman Catholicism, he says, 'Were it not for this voice, speaking so clearly in my conscience and my heart, I should be an atheist, or a pantheist, or a polytheist when I looked into the world.'[9] This reference to the heart as well as the conscience suggests that Newman did not confine an experiential awareness of God to the moral life. It seems rather the case that he regarded the argument from conscience as the most effective *philosophical* argument, not that he did not also think that there were other compelling reasons for believing in God's existence apart from the traditional proofs and evidences.

This is shown very vividly in *Callista* where the pagan heroine is deeply impressed by the fact that the different Christians she meets all make Christianity 'consist in the intimate Divine Presence in the heart':

It was the friendship or mutual love of person with person. Here was the very teaching which already was so urgently demanded both by her reason and her heart, which she found nowhere else; which she found existing one and the same in a female slave, in a country youth, in a learned priest.[10]

In other words, what really draws Callista to the Christian faith is not primarily her awareness of conscience but of the deepest need of the human heart, which cannot ultimately be satisfied by another human person but only by the Person of God.

Indeed, what makes Callista receptive to hearing the gospel in the first place is not a guilty conscience but a profound sense of personal unfulfilment:

'Here am I a living, breathing woman, with an overflowing heart, with keen affections, with a yearning after some object which may possess me. I cannot exist without something to rest upon. I cannot fall back upon that drear, forlorn state, which philosophers call wisdom, and moralists call virtue . . . I must have something to love; love is my life.'[11]

In answer to her objection to the doctrine of hell, Cecilius the priest shows that far from the dogma being an obstacle to faith it is actually involved in Callista's own existential understanding. For if there is a life after death, then

'you will still be *you*. You will still be the same being, but deprived of those outward stays and solaces, which, such as they are, you now enjoy. You will be yourself, shut up in yourself. I have heard that people go mad at length when placed in solitary confinement. If, then, on passing hence, you are cut off from what you had here, and have only the company of yourself, I think your burden will be, so far, greater, not less than it is now . . .'

'Assuming, then, first, that the soul always needs external objects to rest upon; next, that it has no prospect of any such when it leaves this visible scene; and thirdly, that the hunger and thirst, the gnawing of the heart, where it occurs, is as keen and piercing as a flame; it will follow there is nothing irrational in the notion of an eternal Tartarus.'

But if, on the other hand, Cecilius argues, on exactly the same existential lines as Callista,

'all your thoughts go one way; if you have needs, desires, aims, aspirations, all of which demand an Object, and imply, by their very existence, that such an Object does exist also; and if nothing here does satisfy them, and if there be a message which professes to come from that Object, of whom you already have the presentiment, and to teach you about Him, and to bring the remedy you crave; and if those who try that remedy say with one voice that the remedy answers; are you not bound, Callista, at least to look that way, to inquire into what you hear about it, and to ask for His help, if He be, to enable you to believe in Him?'[12]

The argument from conscience already quoted only appears towards the end of the novel just prior to Callista's conversion, and here too it is part – albeit a major part – of a more general awareness of the 'Person she was seeking for': 'Here was that to which her intellect tended, though that intellect could not frame it. It could approve and acknowledge, when set before it, what it could not originate. Here was He who spoke to her in her conscience; whose Voice she heard . . .'[13]

Without this Person life on earth is portrayed by Newman as a kind of living hell for anyone who has, like Callista, the capacity both to love to the full and to be aware of that need. The hellish fate for the heart deprived of the supreme object of love is in effect Newman's definition of hell: ' "You cannot escape from yourself!" '[14] And so Callista is drawn to the Christian God not just because of the voice echoing in her conscience, but because 'the more she thought over what she heard of Christianity, the more she was drawn to it, and the more it approved itself to her whole soul, and the more it seemed to respond to all her needs and aspirations . . .'[15]

Aidan Nichols is disappointed by the *Grammar of Assent*, since, 'Having held out to us the appropriate form for argument to God's existence, a form at once rational and imaginative, Newman's content seems thin gruel in comparison.' For while conceding that the moral argument for the existence of God is not 'dead', Nichols rejects the notion that 'moral experience alone' can provide a basis for belief in God.[16] As already indicated, there are three answers to this criticism: first, Newman does not restrict the relevant human experience for theistic belief to moral experience; second, he does, however, regard, like Kant, the moral argument as the best *philosophical* argument; third, it is a well-known fact that it is the human sense of sin which is the most universal ground *in fact* for religion. It is precisely this feeling of guilt that Newman says in the last chapter of the *Grammar of Assent* is the basis of natural religion, which 'is founded in one way or other on the sense of sin; and without that vivid sense it would hardly have any precepts or any observances'. The fact that God appears to be so strikingly absent from his world is another very good reason why Newman stresses the moral argument:

> I see only a choice of alternatives in explanation of so critical a fact:- either there is no Creator, or He has disowned His creatures. Are then the dim shadows of His Presence in the affairs of men but a fancy of our own, or, on the other hand, has He hid His face and the light of His countenance, because we have in some special way dishonoured Him? My true informant, my burdened conscience, gives me at once the true answer to each of these antagonist questions:– it pronounces without any misgiving that God exists:– and it pronounces quite as surely that I am alienated from Him . . .

It is, after all, the eloquent silence of God which is the most fundamental argument against his existence:

It is a silence that speaks. It is as if others had got possession of His work. Why does not He, our Maker and Ruler, give us some immediate knowledge of Himself? Why does He not write His Moral Nature in large letters upon the face of history, and bring the blind, tumultuous rush of its events into a celestial, hierarchical order? Why does He not grant us in the structure of society at least so much of a revelation of Himself as the religions of the heathen attempt to supply? Why from the beginning of time has no one uniform steady light guided all families of the earth, and all individual men, how to please Him? Why is it possible without absurdity to deny His will, His attributes, His existence? Why does He not walk with us one by one, as He is said to have walked with His chosen men of old time? We both see and know each other; why, if we cannot have the sight of Him, have we not at least the knowledge? On the contrary, He is specially 'a Hidden God'; and with our best efforts we can only glean from the surface of the world some faint and fragmentary views of him.[17]

But it is conscience which provides the answer to the objection, as Newman had already made plain in the last chapter of the *Apologia*, where again he had evoked the sense of the absence of God with an eloquence of which an atheist would be proud:

> ... I look out of myself into the world of men, and there I see a sight which fills me with unspeakable distress. The world seems simply to give the lie to that great truth, of which my whole being is so full; and the effect upon me is, in consequence, as a matter of necessity, as confusing as if it denied that I am in existence myself. If I looked into a mirror, and did not see my face, I should have the sort of feeling which actually comes upon me, when I look into this living busy world, and see no reflexion of its Creator ... I am far from denying the real force of the arguments in proof of a God, drawn from the general facts of human society and the course of history, but these do not warm me or

enlighten me: they do not take away the winter of my desolation, or make the buds unfold and the leaves grow within me, and my moral being rejoice. The sight of the world is nothing else than the prophet's scroll, full of 'lamentations, and mourning, and woe'.

In response to this 'profound mystery, which is absolutely beyond human solution', Newman answers, 'either there is no Creator, or this living society of men is in a true sense discarded from His presence'. But since, in words already quoted, Newman cannot ignore that 'voice' which speaks 'so clearly in my conscience and my heart', it is after all conscience that explains the human condition by making us aware of original sin.[18]

Although, however, Newman surely rightly regards the moral argument from conscience as absolutely basic and integral to any kind of theism, he does, as I have tried to show, possess a wider sense of the human heart and its reasons for believing in a personal God. To appreciate this, we need to turn away from his more formal philosophical and theological writing, not to a novel this time but to his pastoral preaching.

In one of the finest sermons he ever preached, 'The Thought of God, the Stay of the Soul' (1837), Newman, as the title suggests, maintains in effect that a true humanism implies theism. The more deeply we understand human nature the more we see that its ultimate needs demand a divine fulfilment. Without God, the human person 'has faculties and affections without a ruling principle, object, or purpose'. Arguing that 'the happiness of the soul consists in the exercise of the affections', then 'here is at once a reason for saying that the thought of God, and nothing short of it, is the happiness of man', for 'the affections require a something more vast and more enduring than anything created'.[19] We are reminded of St Augustine's famous words, 'our hearts are restless till they rest in you',[20] when we read the equivalent in Newman: 'He alone is sufficient for the heart who made it.' Other human beings cannot satisfy us, partly because they are transient and unreliable in their frailty: 'our hearts require something more permanent and uniform than man can be ... Do not all men die? are they not taken from us? are they not as uncertain as the grass of the field?' But even apart from this, 'there is another reason why God alone is the happiness of our souls', as Newman explains:

> the contemplation of Him, and nothing but it, is able fully to open and relieve the mind, to unlock, occupy, and fix our affections. We may indeed love things created with great intenseness, but such affection, when disjoined from the love of the Creator, is like a stream running in a narrow channel, impetuous, vehement, turbid. The heart runs out, as it were, only at one door; it is not an expanding of the whole man. Created natures cannot open us, or elicit the ten thousand mental senses which belong to us, and through which we really live. None but the presence of our Maker can enter us; for to none besides can the whole heart in all its thoughts and feelings be unlocked and subjected.

The friendship and sympathy of those closest to us cannot rival the intimacy we can enjoy with God alone:

> It is this feeling of simple and absolute confidence and communion, which soothes and satisfies those to whom it is vouchsafed. We know that even our nearest friends enter into us but partially, and hold intercourse with us only at times; whereas the consciousness of a perfect and enduring Presence, and it alone, keeps the heart open.

It is God, then, who liberates the human heart by freeing it from the imprisonment of self:

> Withdraw the Object on which it rests, and it will relapse again into its state of confinement and constraint; and in proportion as it is limited, either to certain seasons or to certain affections, the heart is straightened and distressed. If it be not over bold to say it, He who is infinite can alone be its measure; He alone can answer

to the mysterious assemblage of feelings and thoughts which it has within it.

This is why true happiness depends on belief in God, as otherwise 'We are pent up within ourselves, and are therefore miserable':

> we need a relief to our hearts, that they may be dark and sullen no longer, or that they may not go on feeding upon themselves; we need to escape from ourselves to something beyond; and much as we may wish it otherwise, and may try to make idols to ourselves, nothing short of God's presence is our true refuge; everything else is either a mockery, or but an expedient useful for its season or in its measure.[21]

In *Callista* Newman was writing on the level of practical apologetics; here he is writing in a spiritual vein. But what is so striking is how, outside the philosophical context, it is not the existence of conscience that demands the existence of God but rather it is the ego that is depicted as finding liberation from its own self-imprisonment in the only object external to itself which can offer personal fulfilment, for the plain psychological reason that a person cannot properly 'live without an object' – and so either we live in the unhappiness of the prison of our own ego or we try vainly to find self-fulfilment in other ephemeral finite beings and things. Thus a person

> fancies that he is sufficient for himself; or he supposes that knowledge is sufficient for his happiness; or that exertion, or that the good opinion of others, or (what is called) fame, or that the comforts and luxuries of wealth, are sufficient for him. What a truly wretched state is that coldness and dryness of soul, in which so many live and die. Many a great man, many a peasant, many a busy man, lives and dies with closed heart, with affections undeveloped, unexercised. You see the poor man, passing day after day, Sunday after Sunday, year after year, without a thought in his mind, to appearance almost like a stone. You see the educated man, full of

thought, full of intelligence, full of action, but still with a stone heart, as cold and dead as regards his affections, as if he were the poor ignorant countryman. You see others, with warm affections, perhaps, for their families, with benevolent feelings towards their fellow-men, yet stopping there; centring their hearts on what is sure to fail them, as being perishable. Life passes, riches fly away, popularity is fickle, the senses decay, the world changes, friends die. One alone is constant; One alone is true to us; One alone can be true; One alone can be all things to us; One alone can supply our needs; One alone can train us up to our full perfection; One alone can give a meaning to our complex and intricate nature; One alone can give us tune and harmony; One alone can form and possess us.[22]

Although it is not the moral argument that Newman relies on in either the novel or the sermon, but what we might call the *affective* argument, nevertheless we should not rigidly separate the two, as Newman indicates in a passage in another sermon where he places conscience within the larger context of the whole human person:

There is a voice within us, which assures us that there is something higher than earth. We cannot analyze, define, contemplate what it is that thus whispers to us. It has no shape or material form. There is that in our hearts which prompts us to religion, and which condemns and chastises sin. And this yearning of our nature is met and sustained, it finds an object to rest upon, when it hears of the existence of an All-powerful, All-gracious Creator.[23]

It looks as if Newman chose to stress the strictly moral element in his more philosophical writings, as apparently offering more of a formal *proof* of God's existence, while in his more informal works he emphasises rather the implications and significance of the 'affections and aspirations pent up within' the human heart.[24]

What is really fundamental to Newman's approach to the

existence of God is the existence of the self. It is when we begin to understand the true nature of the human person that we begin to understand that there must be a personal God. This at any rate was how Newman felt in the depths of his being when in his youth he rested 'in the thought of two and two only absolute and luminously self-evident beings, myself and my Creator'.[25] But in one of his Anglican sermons he recognized it was more normal to 'look off from self to the things around us, and forget ourselves in them'. The self either has to turn in on itself or seek some external reality to rest in, and in its fallen state humankind naturally inclines to 'depending for support on the reeds which are no stay, and overlooking our real strength'. But disillusion with the world can turn the self to its true and only source of happiness, when we come to realize 'We still crave for something, we do not well know what; but we are sure it is something which the world has not given us.' And Newman powerfully evokes a sense of transitory vanity of the things of this world:

> And then its changes are so many, so sudden, so silent, so continual. It never leaves changing; it goes on to change, till we are quite sick at heart:– then it is that our reliance on it is broken. It is plain we cannot continue to depend on it, unless we keep pace with it, and go on changing too; but this we cannot do. We feel that, while it changes, we are one and the same . . . and we begin, by degrees, to perceive that there are but two beings in the whole universe, our own soul, and the God who made it.[26]

We could really argue from Newman's works as a whole that he puts as much emphasis on the deep need of the person for relationship with other persons and on the impossibility, aside from the infinite Person of God, of the kind of self-fulfilment that human nature seems to crave, as he does on the implications of conscience. It is above all the affectivity of the human person that Newman wants to emphasize: the need to love and to be loved, the need for a mutual sympathy that cannot be broken and that is all-satisfying: 'the soul of man is made for the contemplation of its Maker; and . . . nothing short of that high contemplation is its happiness'. And 'if we are allowed to find that real and most sacred Object on which our heart may fix itself, a fullness of peace will follow, which nothing but it can give'.[27]

3

THE PERSON OF JESUS CHRIST

In the *Grammar of Assent*, Newman maintains that Christianity alone of the religions of the world 'tends to fulfil the aspirations, needs, and foreshadowings' of theism.[1] This is because he sees the fullness of human self-fulfilment as inseparable from the person of Jesus Christ, 'who fulfils the one great need of human nature, the Healer of its wounds, the Physician of the soul'. It is, then, the idea or image of Christ 'which both creates faith, and then rewards it'. For Christ, who is the 'moral life' of Christians, 'is also the original instrument of their conversion'.[2]

Theism or natural religion is founded on a sense of sin, 'but it cannot find, it does but look out for the remedy'. Christianity, on the other hand, 'has with it that gift of staunching and healing the one deep wound of human nature . . . and therefore it must last while human nature lasts. It is a living truth which never can grow old'. For it is only the redeeming Christ who is the 'remedy, both for guilt and for moral impotence'.[3]

The simple undogmatic, unsacramental Bible Christianity in which Newman had been brought up had one significant advantage over the Catholicism that Newman encountered in the nineteenth-century Roman Catholic Church: it conveyed the vivid image of the Christ of the gospels.

> This is why we see such multitudes in France and Italy giving up religion altogether. They have not impressed upon their hearts the life of our Lord and Saviour as given us in the Evangelists. They believe merely with the intellect, not with the heart. Argument may overset

a mere assent of the reason, but not a faith founded in a personal love for the Object of Faith.[4]

To the question, how do we learn how to love God, he answered simply in one of his Catholic sermon notes, 'By reading of our Lord in the Gospels.'[5]

When he was a member of the Church of England, Newman was highly critical of its powerful Evangelical wing, and one of his most telling criticisms was directed against an introspective rather than christocentric spirituality: 'Instead of looking off to Jesus, and thinking little of ourselves, it is at present thought necessary ... to examine the heart with a view of ascertaining whether it is in a spiritual state or no.' He thought that the 'inherent mischief' of the Evangelical preoccupation with the theory of justification by faith lay 'in its necessarily involving a continual self-contemplation and reference to self'.

> He who aims at attaining sound doctrine or right practice, more or less looks out of himself; whereas, in labouring after a certain frame of mind, there is an habitual reflex action of the mind upon itself ... for, as if it were not enough for a man to look up simply to Christ for salvation, it is declared to be necessary that he should be able to recognize this in himself ... [6]

It was not that Newman was not in his own preaching insistent on the need for self-examination, but he thought that this must never be at the expense of a christocentric spirituality: 'No harm can follow from contemplating our sins, so that we keep Christ before us ...' The danger was when someone 'imprisons himself in his own thoughts, and rests on the workings of his own mind ... instead of putting self aside, and living upon Him who speaks in the Gospels'.[7] There was another related reason why popular Evangelicalism did not seem to Newman to stress Christ enough and that was the result of its concentration on the doctrine of the atonement, that is, upon Christ's work rather than his person. This encouraged what Newman called 'a certain disproportionate attention to the doctrines connected with

the work of Christ, in comparison of those which relate to
His Person', as well as a tendency 'to view the doctrines of
Atonement and Sanctification as the essence of the Gospel'
and to regard the gospels as speaking 'merely of divine
operations, not of Persons'. It was not surprising that Evangelicals spoke more of St Paul's letter to the Romans (where
they found the doctrine of justification by faith) than they
did of the gospels themselves: 'In short, is not the rich and
varied Revelation of our merciful Lord practically reduced
to a few chapters of St Paul's Epistles . . .?'[8] If everything
depended on Christ's saving death on the cross, then his
incarnate person and the rest of his earthly life, not to
mention his resurrection, ascension, and return in the Holy
Spirit at Pentecost, were not surprisingly relegated to comparative insignificance. Evangelicals preached continuously,
Newman complained, about the so-called 'Christian
motives', that is, 'the motives of gratitude' for the atonement; whereas what Newman wanted was 'Christ set forth
from the first as the object of our worship'.[9] He intended his
own sermons to be above all else 'real', to have 'reality in
them', by bringing out the gospels in all their concrete
actuality.[10] His aim as a preacher was to depict the person
of Christ not in an 'unreal way – as a mere idea or vision',
but as 'Scripture has set Him before us in His actual sojourn
on earth, in His gestures, words, and deeds'. Instead of using
'vague statements about His love, His willingness to receive
the sinner, His imparting repentance and spiritual aid, and
the like', Newman's sermons try to present 'Christ as manifested in the Gospels, the Christ who exists therein, external
to our own imaginings . . . really a living being'.[11]

In one of his posthumously published meditations,
Newman points out that while John the Baptist 'was separated from the world', Jesus himself came into this world
not 'in any shape or capacity or office which was above the
course of ordinary human life – not as a Nazarene, not as a
Levitical priest, not as a monk, not as a hermit, but in
the fulness and exactness of human nature'. In view of the
commonly-voice criticism that Newman's high Alexandrian
christology meant that he paid only a notional attention to

the humanity of Christ,[12] it is remarkable to read in this meditation a fulsome celebration of the human Jesus, concluding in the assertion that Jesus was actually *more* human than any human being:

> Thou comest not only a perfect man, but as proper man; not formed anew out of earth, not with the spiritual body which Thou now hast, but in that very flesh which had fallen in Adam, and with all our infirmities, all our feelings and sympathies, sin excepted . . .
>
> O dearest Lord, Thou art more fully man than the holy Baptist, than St John, Apostle and Evangelist, than Thy own sweet Mother. As in Divine knowledge of me Thou art beyond them all, so also in experience and personal knowledge of my nature. Thou art my elder brother.[13]

The fact is that although no one was more insistent on the divinity of Christ against the liberal Protestant tendency to downplay or even question it, no one was more anxious to emphasize the reality of the incarnation, whereby Jesus Christ took to himself our human nature, not 'as something distinct and separate from Himself, but as simply, absolutely, eternally His, so as to be included by us in the very thought of Him'.[14] By taking the incarnation as his starting-point, Newman separated himself from the generality of Western Christians who saw the cross of Christ as the heart of Christianity, whether in terms of the Protestant doctrine of the atonement or from the Catholic perspective of the sacrifice of the Mass. Near the beginning of the *Essay on the Development of Christian Doctrine* (1845), Newman says that if one was looking for the ' "leading idea" . . . of Christianity', around which other ideas could be grouped simply 'for convenience', then he would personally 'call the Incarnation the central aspect of Christianity, out of which the three main aspects of its teaching take their rise, the sacramental, the hierarchical, and the ascetic'. It is true that he immediately modifies this by adding, 'But one aspect of Revelation must not be allowed to exclude or to obscure another'. However, later in the book, he writes, cautiously again: 'For the convenience of arrangement, I will consider the Incarnation as the central truth of the gospel, and the source whence we are to draw out its principles'.[15] This was certainly not the approach of what Newman called 'the popular theology of the day' which stressed the atonement as 'the chief doctrine of the Gospel'. Rather, Newman's own natural preference for giving priority to the incarnation is to be attributed to the influence of the Greek Fathers with their deeply incarnational theology. This, as we shall see, is only one aspect of a theological personalism which Newman derived from his early systematic reading of the early Fathers.[16] From his patristic studies he learned that the incarnation was not simply a means to the crucifixion but a salvific event in itself since God took to himself human nature in order that he might raise it to the divine level, that is, 'deify' it, so as 'to make us partakers of the Divine nature'. In other words, God became man so that 'men, through brotherhood with Him, might in the end become as gods', to use the word that the Fathers themselves dared to use. Thus human nature was 'renewed' in Christ, 'glorious and wonderful beyond our thoughts'.[17] For he 'came, selecting and setting apart for Himself the elements of body and soul; then, uniting them to Himself from their first origin of existence, pervading them, hallowing them by His own Divinity, spiritualizing them, and filling them with light and purity, the while they continued to be human ... And as they grew from day to day in their holy union, His eternal Essence still was one with them, exalting them'.[18]

As a Catholic, Newman did not hesitate to ally himself with the view of Duns Scotus (as against St Thomas Aquinas) that even if human beings had never sinned, the Son of God would still have 'had it in mind to come on earth among innocent creatures ... to fill them with ... grace, to receive their worship, to enjoy their company, and to prepare them for ... heaven'. Newman was convinced that there would have been an incarnation, although it would have taken a different form, without the fall: 'He once had meant to come on earth in heavenly glory, but we sinned; and then He could not safely visit us, except with a shrouded

radiance and a bedimmed Majesty, for He was God. So He
came Himself in weakness, not in power.'[19] The idea of a
personal God seemed almost to demand a personal manifes-
tation in human form: how otherwise could there be a
mutual relation of love? This at any rate was what commended the incarnation to Callista:

> 'We have no love for Him who alone lasts. We love those
> things which do not last, but come to an end. Things
> being thus, He whom we ought to love has determined
> to win us back to Him. With this Object He has come
> into His own world, in the form of one of us men. And
> in that human form He opens His arms and woos us to
> return to Him, our Maker'.

It was not simply that Callista was drawn to a particular
religious view of life, to Christianity: it was by the incarnate
person of the personal God which she had discovered in
the gospels that she was irresistibly fascinated.

> Here was that to which her intellect tended, though
> that intellect could not frame it. It could approve and
> acknowledge, when set before it, what it could not orig-
> inate. Here was He who spoke to her in her conscience;
> whose Voice she heard, whose Person she was seeking
> for . . . That image sank deep into her; she felt it to be
> a reality.[20]

Ultimately, what must attract people to Christianity, Newman
thought, was not so much Christianity as the person of
Christ, the incarnate Son of God. It was the concrete image
that made the personal rapport possible between the personal God and the individual believer.

Having said that the incarnation rather than the crucifixion was at the heart of Newman's spirituality, it is worth
looking at two sermons where he makes the person of Christ
come alive in the passion of the cross. The first sermon,
'The Incarnate Son, a Sufferer and Sacrifice' (1836), was
recalled in a well-known passage by an eye-witness, the historian James Anthony Froude, who had heard it preached
in the university church of St Mary the Virgin at the height

of the Oxford Movement. Froude's account is not exactly accurate, but is worth quoting to show the deeply personal effect Newman's preaching had on his congregation.

Having, according to Froude, 'described closely some of the incidents of our Lord's passion', Newman then 'paused':

> For a few minutes there was a breathless silence. Then, in a low, clear voice, of which the faintest vibration was audible in the farthest corner of St Mary's, he said, 'Now, I bid you recollect that He to whom these things were done was Almighty God.' It was as if an electric stroke had gone through the church, as if every person present understood for the first time the meaning of what he had all his life been saying. I suppose it was an epoch in the mental history of more than one of my Oxford contemporaries.[21]

In actual fact the dramatic moment came after Newman had been insisting that God did suffer on the cross not in his divine but in his human nature – 'God the Son suffered *in* that human nature which He had taken to Himself and made His own':

> Think of this, all ye light-hearted, and consider whether with this thought you can read the last chapters of the four Gospels without fear and trembling.
>
> For instance: 'When He had thus spoken, one of the officers which stood by struck Jesus with the palm of his hand, saying, Answerest thou the high priest so?' The words must be said, though I hardly dare say them, – that officer lifted up his hand against God the Son. This is not a figurative way of speaking, or a rhetorical form of words, or a harsh, extreme, and unadvisable statement; it is a literal and simple truth, it is a great Catholic doctrine.[22]

Although the passage is ostensibly about the passion of Christ, it is of course really about his incarnation, the reality of which Newman realized in that pregnant pause and those dreadful words, 'that officer lifted up his hand against God the Son,' which made such a deep impression on the young

Froude. It was all very well to speak in a general kind of way about the incarnation of God, but for Newman the *real* as opposed to *notional* understanding of the doctrine meant that it was important to draw out the concrete implications in as personal a way as possible: it was because the Word had become flesh in a particular Jew living in a particular place at a particular time that it was possible for a mere creature actually to hit his Creator.

If we now turn to one of the best of his Catholic sermons, which bears comparison with the best of his Anglican ones, the remarkable 'Mental Sufferings of Our Lord in His Passion', published in *Discourses Addressed to Mixed Congregations* (1849), we find the actual pain of the crucifixion evoked with extraordinary empathy and realism. It does not content Newman merely to dwell on the physical agony of the long-drawn-out death by asphyxiation of a Roman crucifixion; indeed Newman indicates that Christ died unusually soon from that peculiarly cruel execution because he died from mental rather than physical causes. Newman's question now is: if Jesus was really and truly God incarnate, then what must have been the true nature of the passion, given that he also shared our humanity? Again, Newman switches the spotlight on the person of the historical Christ, in his unique combination of divine personality and human nature. He insists on realizing for his hearers who it was that suffered and how he suffered. And in doing so he illuminates the mystery of how Jesus Christ could be both God and man at one and the same time.

He begins by pointing out that since Jesus was truly human he had a soul as well as a body. His suffering therefore was also completely human since human pain is not just physical but also spiritual – 'there is no real pain, though there may be apparent suffering, when there is no kind of inward sensibility or spirit to be the seat of it'. Animals cannot feel pain in the same way that human beings do 'because they cannot reflect on what they feel; they have no advertence or direct consciousness of their sufferings. This is it that makes pain so trying, viz., that we cannot help thinking of it, while we suffer it.' This is why, Newman argues with considerable psychological acumen, human beings in intense agony feel

> that they have borne *as much* as they can bear; as if the continuance and not the intenseness was what made it too much for them. What does this mean, but that the memory of the foregoing moments of pain acts upon and (as it were) edges the pain that succeeds? If the third or fourth or twentieth moment of pain could be taken by itself, if the succession of the moments that preceded it could be forgotten, it would be no more than the first moment, as bearable as the first (taking away the shock which accompanies the first); but what makes it unbearable is, that it *is* the twentieth ... It is the intellectual comprehension of pain, as a whole diffused through successive moments, which gives it its special power and keenness, and it is the soul only, which a brute has not, which is capable of that comprehension.

Newman now applies his analogy to the suffering of Christ:

> Do you recollect their offering Him wine mingled with myrrh, when He was on the point of being crucified? He would not drink of it; why? because such a potion would have stupified His mind, and He was bent on bearing the pain in all its bitterness ... He did not turn away His face from the suffering; He confronted it, or, as I may say, He breasted it, that every particular portion of it might make its due impression on Him. And as men are superior to brute animals, and are affected by pain more than they, by reason of the mind within them, which gives a substance to pain, such as it cannot have in the instance of brutes; so, in like manner, our Lord felt pain of the body, with an advertence and a consciousness, and therefore with a keenness and intensity, and with a unity of perception, which none of us can possibly fathom or compass, because His soul was so absolutely in His power, so simply free from the influence of distractions, so fully directed *upon* the pain,

so utterly surrendered, so simply subjected to the suffering. And thus He may truly be said to have suffered the whole of His passion in every moment of it.[23]

Newman may seem practically to deny the humanity of Christ when he says that Christ was in complete control of his passion:

> The soul of other men is subjected to its own wishes, feelings, impulses, passions, perturbations; His soul was subjected simply to His Eternal and Divine Personality. Nothing happened to His soul by chance, or on a sudden; He never was taken by surprise; nothing affected Him without His willing beforehand that it should affect Him.

But what is so striking is that the conclusion Newman draws from the fully voluntary nature of Christ's suffering is that Christ suffered *in his humanity* far more than he could have done if he had been *only* a human being. In other words, instead of his divinity diminishing his pain on the cross, it actually caused a thoroughly human pain utterly in excess of anything we can conceive of. To the obvious objection that Christ could not have suffered as much as an ordinary human being would if he was the Son of God and knew he was, Newman's reply is that the opposite was true, namely that Christ suffered so much in his humanity precisely because of his divinity.

> As the whole of His body, stretched out upon the Cross, so the whole of His soul, His whole advertence, His whole consciousness, a mind awake, a sense acute, a living co-operation, a present, absolute intention, not a virtual permission, not a heartless submission, this did He present to His tormentors. His passion was an action; He lived most energetically, while He lay languishing, fainting, and dying. Nor did He die, except by an act of the will; for He bowed His head, in command as well as in resignation, and said, 'Father, into Thy hands I commend My spirit;' He gave the word, He surrendered His soul, He did not lose it.

The last two sentences might seem to impugn the reality of Christ's humanity, but Newman is clear and emphatic that this is not the case:

> God was the sufferer; God suffered in His human nature; the sufferings belonged to God, and were drunk up, were drained out to the bottom of the chalice, because God drank them; not tasted or sipped, not flavoured, disguised by human medicaments, as man disposes of the cup of anguish.

Just as human suffering is greater than animal suffering because of human consciousness, so Christ's passion was of an extraordinary nature because of its unique psychological character – 'He walks forth into a mental agony with as definite an action as if it were some bodily torture.' Christ's suffering, Newman claims, was essentially mental rather than bodily suffering. In answer to the argument that one would expect Christ to 'be supported under His trial by the consciousness of innocence and the anticipation of triumph', Newman contends that in fact 'his trial consisted in the withdrawal, as of other causes of consolation, so of that very consciousness and anticipation'. And 'as men of self-command can turn from one thought to another at their will, so much more did He deliberately deny Himself the comfort, and satiate Himself with the woe'.

Having argued that Christ's psychological suffering was uniquely painful, Newman now comes to the paradoxical conclusion that the actual experience that caused such terrible anguish was the kind of experience that ordinary human beings experience with comparative indifference:

> He had to bear what is well known to us, what is familiar to us, but what to Him was woe unutterable. He had to bear that which is so easy a thing to us, so natural, so welcome, that we cannot conceive of it as of a great endurance, but which to Him had the scent and the poison of death – He had . . . to bear the weight of sin . . . He had to bear the sin of the whole world.

And Newman concludes the sermon by attributing Christ's

death not to physical causes but to mental suffering: 'And then, when the appointed moment arrived, and He gave the word, as His Passion had begun with His soul, with the soul did it end. He did not die of bodily exhaustion, or of bodily pain; at His will His tormented Heart broke, and He commended His Spirit to the Father.[24]

It is worth noticing that this sermon which so vividly depicted the inner mental life of Christ had almost certainly an influence on one of Gerard Manley Hopkins's 'Terrible Sonnets', beginning 'No worst, there is none', where the marvellous line 'More pangs will, schooled at forepangs, wilder wring' exactly echoes Newman's thought.[25] But it is hardly surprising that it should have had such an impact on a poetic sensibility so preoccupied with the individual and the concrete. Newman the preacher had no time for vague abstractions and generalities: as we have seen, he saw it as his duty to represent the living person of Christ who is the inspiration of the individual Christian. For it is the personal relationship with the Lord that must be at the heart of Christianity.

One particular characteristic of the Christ of the gospels that Newman noted, as we have seen, in 'Mental Sufferings of Our Lord in His Passion' is his *calmness*. It is a trait that strongly engaged his imagination. Thus, for example, he contrasts the attitude of Jesus as his death approached and that of his disciples and the Jews:

> *He* steadily fixing His face to endure those sufferings which were the atonement for our sins, yet without aught of mental excitement or agitation; His disciples and the Jewish multitude first protesting their devotion to Him in vehement language, then, the one deserting Him, the other even clamouring for His crucifixion.

The Lord's prayer itself, Newman suggests, is typical: 'How plain and unadorned is it! How few are the words of it! How grave and solemn the petitions! What an entire absence of tumult and feverish emotion!' Even in the garden of Gethsemane, when he 'was in distress of mind beyond our understanding', and was praying the cup might pass from him, 'how subdued and how concise is His petition!'[26] Of course, Newman had his reasons in his Anglican preaching for emphasizing this characteristic of Christ, as, in contradistinction to the emotionalism of Evangelical Christianity, he wanted to maintain that the hallmark of a mature Christian spirituality is a deep calmness: 'the highest Christian temper is free from all vehement and tumultuous feeling'. The proof is again the figure of Christ himself as portrayed in the gospels: 'When does He set us an example of passionate devotion, of enthusiastic wishes, or of intemperate words?'[27]

Christ is also seen by Newman as displaying that favourite Tractarian virtue of reserve in his dealing with people. Far from seeking recognition, Jesus ordered those he encountered not to publicize his deeds, 'as if what is called popularity would be a dishonour to His holy name, and the applause of men would imply their right to censure':

> He spoke as one who knew He had great favours to confer, and had nothing to gain from those who received them. Far from urging them to accept His bounty, He showed Himself even backward to confer it, inquired into their knowledge and motives, and cautioned them against entering His service without counting the cost of it. Thus sometimes He even repelled men from Him.[28]

It is not just that Newman wanted to make the person of Christ real to his hearers; he was also well aware of the perennial tendency of every age and society to look at Jesus from the perspective of their own concerns and preoccupations: 'The world . . . in every age . . . chooses some one or other peculiarity of the Gospel as the badge of its particular fashion for the time being . . .' In a modern civilized society which prides itself on its compassion and regard for human rights, there is the danger of too soft a Christianity, lacking in 'firmness, manliness, godly severity'. Newman thought that this deficiency led to a distortion of the virtue of charity, in so far as an 'element of zeal and holy sternness' was needed 'to temper and give character to the languid, unmeaning benevolence which we misname Christian love'.[29]

Newman's Jesus is not only the Christ of compassion, the 'caring' Christ, but also the Christ who drove out the money-lenders from the Temple with cords. It is the same Christ who inspires both fear and love, who felt affection for the rich young man in the gospel story but also made the severest of demands on him. Thus Christ 'loves us, yet speaks harshly to us that we may learn to cherish mixed feelings towards Him. He hides Himself from us, and yet calls on us, that we may hear His voice as Samuel did, and, believing, approach Him with trembling.'

In the same way for the Christian, *'fear and love must go together'*, Newman insists. There is no room in his spirituality for any kind of easy familiarity with an indulgent, avuncular kind of God:

> No one can love God aright without fearing Him; though many fear Him, and yet do not love Him. Self-confident men, who do not know their own hearts, or the reasons they have for being dissatisfied with themselves, do not fear God, and they think this bold freedom is to love Him. Deliberate sinners fear but cannot love Him . . . No one really loves another, who does not feel a certain reverence towards him.[30]

It is a message, however unpopular, that Newman never tires of repeating: 'The fear of God is the beginning of wisdom . . . Fear and love must go together; always fear, always love, to your dying day . . . Till you know what it is to fear with the terrified sailors or the Apostles, you cannot sleep with Christ at your Heavenly Father's feet.'

But the paradoxical point that Newman wants to make is that the more we understand Christ's love, the more we shall in fact fear him because the more we shall feel our own unworthiness. Thus, while he insists, 'you must always fear while you hope,' he explains this by adding, 'Your knowledge of your sins increases with your view of God's mercy in Christ.'[31]

Newman had other surprises, too, for his congregation as

he tried to undermine their stereotyped ideas by representing to them the concrete figure of Christ in the gospels. The popular notion that Christ was a radical who ignored and swept aside accepted religious forms is hardly compatible with his 'dutiful attention to the religious system under which He was born; and that, not only so far as it was directly divine, but further, where it was the ordinance of uninspired though pious men, where it was but founded on ecclesiastical authority'. It should be no surprise that he presented himself for baptism to John the Baptist. Certainly his followers 'neither abandoned the Jewish rites themselves, nor obliged any others to do so who were used to them'.[32]

This, of course did not mean that Christ was conventionally, let alone respectably, religious. He was, in fact, Newman points out bluntly, 'what would now be called with contempt a vagrant'.[33] That, at least, was what he was essentially during his active ministry, which lasted only three years. Before that he lived in obscurity in Nazareth until he was thirty. For a certain kind of activist Christian this presents a peculiar problem: 'How very wonderful is all this! that He should live here, doing nothing great, so long; living here, as if for the sake of living; not preaching, or collecting disciples, or apparently in any way furthering the cause which brought Him down from heaven.'

Outwardly quite unremarkable, he had one unique characteristic which went unnoticed because, Newman suggests, it would always go unnoticed:

> He was in all respects a man, except that he did not sin, and this great difference the many would not detect, because none of us understands those who are much better than himself: so that Christ, the sinless of God, might be living close to us, and we not discover it.

Indeed, would *we* have recognized Christ for who he was any more than his contemporaries if he had been 'our next door neighbour, or one of our family'? Would we not have thought him 'strange, eccentric, extravagant, and fanciful'? Newman presses the point home relentlessly: surely we too would have rejected Christ had we been the Jews:

We say, that had we had the advantage of being with Christ, we should have had stronger motives, stronger restraints against sin. I answer, that so far from our sinful habits being reformed by the presence of Christ, the chance is, that those same habits would have hindered us from recognizing Him. We should not have known He was present; and if He had even told us who He was, we should not have believed Him. Nay, had we seen His miracles (incredible as it may seem), even they would not have made any lasting impression on us.

Indeed the terrible fact is that the people who came closest to the earthly Jesus were the very people who rejected him most dreadfully, as Newman explains in one of the most powerful passages in his sermons:

Could men come nearer to God than when they seized Him, struck Him, spit on Him, hurried Him along, stripped Him, stretched out His limbs upon the cross, nailed Him to it, raised it up, stood gazing on Him, jeered Him, gave him vinegar, looked close whether He was dead, and then pierced Him with a spear? O dreadful thought, that the nearest approaches man has made to God upon earth have been in blasphemy! Whether of the two came closer to Him, St. Thomas, who was allowed to reach forth his hand and reverently touch His wounds, and St. John, who rested on His bosom, or the brutal soldiers who profaned Him limb by limb, and tortured Him nerve by nerve? His Blessed Mother, indeed, came closer still to Him; and we, if we be true believers, still closer, who have Him really, though spiritually, within us; but this is another, an inward sort of approach. Of those who approached Him externally, they came nearest, who knew nothing about it.

But Newman is not content with making the point that the Jews behaved no differently from the way in which people in any age would have treated Christ. He wants to impress upon us that actually we are doing exactly what the Jews did to Christ. For Christ has not left this world, but is still present in a different, but similarly hidden mode:

> The Holy Ghost's coming is so really His coming, that we might as well say that He was not here in the days of His flesh, when He was visibly in this world, as deny that He is here now, when He is here by His Divine Spirit . . .
>
> Next, if He is still on earth, yet is not visible (which cannot be denied), it is plain that He keeps Himself still in the condition which He chose in the days of His flesh. I mean, He is a hidden Saviour, and may be approached (unless we are careful) without due reverence and fear . . . It is probable, then, that we can now commit at least as great blasphemy towards Him as the Jews did first, because we are under the dispensation of that Holy Spirit, against whom even more heinous sins *can* be committed; next, because His presence now as little witnesses of itself, or is impressive to the many, as His bodily presence formerly.

This is why sinful Christians now are in a similar situation to those in Christ's own time who came closest to him externally:

> So it is with sinners: they would walk close to the throne of God; they would stupidly gaze at it; they would touch it; they would meddle with the holiest things; they would go on intruding and prying, not meaning any thing wrong by it, but with a sort of brute curiosity, till the avenging lightnings destroyed them; – all because they have no *senses* to guide them in the matter.

For, says Newman, concluding his argument with one of the most arresting – and horrifying – images he ever employed,

> sinners have no spiritual sense; they can presage nothing; they do not know what is going to happen the next moment to them. So they go fearlessly further and further among precipices, till on a sudden they fall, or are smitten and perish. Miserable beings! and this is

what sin does for immortal souls; that they should be like the cattle which are slaughtered at the shambles, yet touch and smell the very weapons which are to destroy them![34]

We shall see later how for Newman sin is not merely the transgression of an impersonal moral law but is rather a personal affront to the person of Christ.

As we have said, Newman regretted the ignorance of the gospels among the Catholics of his day. But he insisted as a Catholic preacher that Catholicism was nothing if it was not the loving contemplation of Christ – that 'energetic, direct apprehension of an unseen Lord and Saviour' which it is the work of the Church to foster in all times among Catholics:

Age passes after age, and she varies her discipline, and she adds to her devotions, and all with the one purpose of fixing her own and their gaze more fully upon the person of her unseen Lord. She has adoringly surveyed Him, feature by feature, and has paid a separate homage to Him in every one. She has made us honour His Five Wounds, His Precious Blood, and His Sacred Heart. She has bid us meditate on His infancy, and the Acts of His ministry; His agony, His scourging, and His crucifixion . . . [35]

In the same sermon Newman puts his finger on the difference between the atmospheres of Catholic and Protestant churches, a difference often felt but not analysed. For Newman the difference is that in a Catholic church the presence of the person of Christ is powerfully present, whereas in a Protestant church it is the doctrine of the atonement (if it is an Evangelical church) that is eloquently preached and fervently believed. In other words, whereas in the one church the word of God is proclaimed, in the other the incarnate Son of God is also sacramentally present through the Eucharist. This explains the spontaneity and lack of embarrassment among Catholic worshippers, a fact often commented on by observers. For whereas Protestants 'are serious at prayer time, and behave with decency . . .

mere duty, a sense of propriety, and good behaviour, these are not the ruling principles present in the mind of our worshippers':

> Wherefore, on the contrary, those spontaneous postures of devotion? why those unstudied gestures? why those abstracted countenances? why that heedlessness of the presence of others? why that absence of the shame-facedness which is so sovereign among professors of other creeds? The spectator sees the effect; he cannot understand the cause of it. *Why* is this simple earnest-ness of worship? *we* have no difficulty in answering. It is because the Incarnate Saviour is present in the tabernacle ... It is the visible Sign of the Son of Man ... [36]

If Catholicism, if Christianity, essentially consists in the contemplation of Christ, this is also the key to its successful propagation. It is Christ who is the cause and ground of faith. In one of his Catholic sermons, 'The Secret Power of Divine Grace' (1856), Newman takes over and adapts a striking passage from an earlier Anglican sermon, 'Invisible Presence of Christ' (1841).[37] There he had preached that the gospel answers a deeply felt need by filling the emptiness of the human heart:

> Man is not sufficient for his own happiness; he is not happy except the Presence of God be with him. When he was created, God breathed into him that supernatu-ral life of the Spirit which is his true happiness: and when he fell, he lost the divine gift, and with it his happiness also. Ever since he has been unhappy; ever since he has a void within him which needs filling, and he knows not how to fill it. He scarcely realizes his own need: only his actions show that he feels it, for he is ever restless when he is not dull and insensible, seeking in one thing or another that blessing which he has lost. Multitudes, indeed, there are, whose minds have never been opened; and multitudes who stupify and deaden their minds, till they lose their natural hunger and

thirst: but, whether aware of their need or not, whether made restless by it or not, still all men have it, and the Gospel supplies it; and then, even if they did not recognize their want by nature, they at length learn it by its supply.

There is no great mystery, then, or riddle about the spread of Christianity: no need to look for hidden causes. The secret of its success is summed up in Newman's marvellous words: 'the keen, vivid, constraining glance of Christ's countenance'.[38] It is not a philosophical or theological abstraction but 'the piercing, soul-subduing look of the Son of Man' who fulfils the otherwise unfulfillable human longing for 'an object of life'.[39]

4

THE CHRISTIAN REVELATION – PERSONAL OR PROPOSITIONAL?

Even after embracing the dogmas of Catholicism, Newman was as emphatic as he had been while an Anglican that the Christian revelation is fundamentally personal rather than propositional, that is to say, constituted by the living person of Christ rather than by doctrinal propositions about him. For God reveals his own self rather than truths about himself. In fact, of course, in the incarnation God reveals himself in the person of Jesus Christ. Thus the revelation of God in Christ is primarily a personal one: 'What Catholics, what Church doctors, as well as Apostles, have ever lived on, is not any number of theological canons or decrees, but . . . the Christ Himself, as He is represented in concrete existence in the Gospels.'[1] What Newman says of Catholic practice agrees with his own approach as an Anglican:

> As God is one, so the impression which He gives us of Himself is one; it is not a thing of parts; it is not a system . . . It is the vision of an object. When we pray, we pray, not to an assemblage of notions, or to a creed, but to One individual Being; and when we speak of Him we speak of a Person . . . This being the case, all our attempts to delineate our impression of Him go to bring out one idea, not two or three or four; not a

philosophy, but an individual idea in its separate aspects.

Our experience of God revealed in Christ is not, of course, an immediate one as it was for the apostles, but is mediated to us through their unique experience of the reality: 'The ideas which we are granted of Divine Objects under the Gospel, from the nature of the case and because they are ideas, answer to the Originals so far as this, that they are whole, indivisible, substantial, and may be called real, as being images of what is real.'[2]

But if it is true that Newman's theology of revelation was fundamentally personalistic rather than propositional, this does not mean that he was in any way anti-dogmatic. First of all, although revelation is above all the revelation of a person, this does not imply that it is merely subjective in a vague kind of way. After all, a person speaks, and 'Why should God speak, unless He meant to say something? Why should He say it, unless He meant us to hear?' If there has been a definitive revelation, then 'there must be some essential doctrine proposed by it to our faith'. In other words, 'Religion cannot but be dogmatic; it ever has been.'[3] Newman is clear that if revelation is a 'vision', it is also a 'message'.[4] For the gospel 'is no mere philosophy thrown upon the world at large, no mere quality of mind and thought, no mere beautiful and deep sentiment or subjective opinion, but a substantive message from above'.[5]

The balance that Newman keeps between the personal and the propositional aspects of revelation extends also to his treatment of dogma. In *The Arians of the Fourth Century* (1833), he took a distinctly negative line. Far from dogmatic formulations being desirable for their own sake, he insists there that 'freedom from symbols and articles is abstractedly the highest state of Christian communion, and the peculiar privilege of the primitive Church', for 'technicality and formalism are, in their degree, inevitable results of public confessions of faith', and 'when confessions do not exist, the mysteries of divine truth, instead of being exposed to the gaze of the profane and uninstructed, are kept hidden in the bosom of the Church, far more faithfully than is otherwise possible'. However, Newman recognizes that dogmatic definitions are both inevitable and necessary, although 'the rulers of the [early] Church were dilatory in applying a remedy, which nevertheless the circumstances of the time imperatively required. They were loath to confess, that the Church had grown too old to enjoy the free, unsuspicious teaching with which her childhood was blest.'[6]

Newman's lack of enthusiasm for dogmatic propositions partly resulted from his awareness of the inadequacy of human language to express revelation, which in turn came from his discovery of the early Church's principle of *economy*. His study of the Alexandrian Church introduced him to the theology of Clement and Origen, which was 'based on the mystical or sacramental principle, and spoke of the various Economies or Dispensations of the Eternal'. Accordingly, the Church's 'mysteries are but the expressions in human language of truths to which the human mind is unequal'.[7] The principle of economy meant that the doctrine of the Trinity, for example, can be seen only as 'the shadow, projected for the contemplation of the intellect, of the Object of scripturally-informed piety: a representation, economical; necessarily imperfect, as being exhibited in a foreign medium, and therefore involving apparent inconsistencies or mysteries'. 'Systematic' dogma could be 'kept in the background in the infancy of Christianity, when faith and obedience were vigorous', and only 'brought forward at a time when, reason being disproportionately developed, and aiming at sovereignty in the province of religion, its presence became necessary to expel an usurping idol from the house of God.' From the point of view of the individual believer, to make explicit what was implicit was not necessarily desirable. 'So reluctant is a well-constituted mind to reflect on its own motive principles, that the correct intellectual image, from its hardness of outline, may startle and offend those who have all along been acting upon it.' But having indicated how undesirable dogmatic formulations are, Newman immediately proceeds to show how necessary they are: for the fact that 'we cannot restrain the rovings of the intellect, or silence its clamorous demand for a formal statement concerning the Object of our worship' means paradoxically that the insistence that 'intellectual representation should ever be subordinate to the cultivation of the religious affections' actually demands the 'intellectual expression of theological truth', not only because it 'excludes heresy', but because it 'directly assists the acts of religious worship and obedience'.[8]

In *Tract 73* (1835), later republished under the title 'On the Introduction of Rationalistic Principles into Revealed Religion', Newman explains why human language is inherently incapable of expressing adequately the truths of divine revelation. 'Considered as a Mystery', a revealed truth 'is doctrine enunciated by inspiration, in human language, as the only possible medium of it, and suitably, according to the capacity of language; a doctrine *lying hid* in language, to be received in that language from the first by every mind, whatever be its separate power of understanding it'. He takes the necessity of verbal formulations for granted, but he also recognizes the inevitable inadequacy of language and the limitations of human thought. He formulates a brilliant exposition of how mystery is involved in the idea of revelation:

> No revelation can be complete and systematic, from the weakness of the human intellect; *so far as* it is not such, it is mysterious . . . A Revelation is religious doctrine viewed on the side unilluminated. Thus Religious Truth is neither light nor darkness, but both together; it is like the dim view of a country seen in the twilight, with forms half extracted from the darkness, with broken lines, and isolated masses. Revelation . . . is not a revealed *system*, but consists of a number of detached and incomplete truths belonging to a vast system unrevealed, of doctrines and injunctions mysteriously connected together.[9]

In *Lectures on the Doctrine of Justification* (1838), doctrinal statements are still seen as negative rather than positive.

Necessary and useful as 'landmarks' and summaries of belief, they are

> intended to forbid speculations, which are sure to spring up in the human mind, and to anticipate its attempts at systematic views by showing the ultimate abyss at which all rightly conducted inquiries arrive, not to tell us anything definite and real, which we did not know before, or which is beyond the faith of the most unlearned.[10]

By the time, however, that Newman came to write the last of the *Oxford University Sermons* on 'The Theory of Developments in Religious Doctrine' (1843), the formulation of dogmatic propositions is viewed in a more positive light, if only because doctrinal development is seen as a sign of life in the Church. It is true that doctrinal statements are said to be 'necessary only because the human mind cannot reflect . . . except piecemeal' upon 'the one idea which they are designed to express', so that they are only expressions of 'aspects' of the 'idea' and 'can never really be confused with the idea itself, which all such propositions taken together can but reach, and cannot exceed', and indeed to which they 'are never equivalent' – for 'dogmas are, after all, but symbols of a Divine fact, which, far from being compassed by those very propositions, would not be exhausted, nor fathomed, by a thousand'. On the other hand dogmatic definitions are regarded as essential for realizing the Christian revelation. There is no contradiction between a personal faith in Christ and a dogmatic creed because the latter only seeks to give expression and substance to the former:

> That idea is not enlarged, if propositions are added, nor impaired if they are withdrawn: if they are added, this is with a view of conveying that one integral view, not of amplifying it. That view does not depend on such propositions: it does not consist in them; they are but specimens and indications of it. And they may be multiplied without limit. They are necessary, but not needful

to it, being but portions or aspects of that previous impression which has at length come under the cognizance of Reason and the terminology of science . . . One thing alone has to be impressed on us by Scripture, the Catholic idea, and in it they are all included. To object, then, to the number of propositions, upon which an anathema is placed, is altogether to mistake their use; for their multiplication is not intended to enforce many things, but to express one.[11]

If this view of revelation (the 'idea') seems too impersonal, then it is important to look at the later passage in the *Grammar of Assent* where Newman provides a classic statement of the relation between a personal faith and doctrinal belief. There he criticizes 'the common mistake of supposing that there is a contrariety and antagonism between a dogmatic creed and vital religion':

People urge that salvation consists, not in believing the propositions that there is a God, that there is a Saviour, that our Lord is God, that there is a Trinity, but in believing in God, in a Saviour, in a Sanctifier; and they object that such propositions are but a formal and human medium destroying all true reception of the Gospel, and making religion a matter of words or of logic, instead of its having its seat in the heart. They are right so far as this, that men can and sometimes do rest in the propositions themselves as expressing intellectual notions; they are wrong, when they maintain that men need do so or always do so. The propositions may and must be used, and can easily be used, as the expression of facts, not notions, and they are necessary to the mind in the same way that language is ever necessary for denoting facts, both for ourselves as individuals, and for our intercourse with others. Again, they are useful in their dogmatic aspect as ascertaining and making clear for us the truths on which the religious imagination has to rest. Knowledge must ever precede the exercise of the affections. We feel gratitude and love, we feel indignation and dislike, when we have the

informations actually put before us which are to kindle
those several emotions. We love our parents, as our
parents, when we know them to be our parents; we
must know concerning God, before we can feel love,
fear, hope, or trust towards Him. Devotion must have
its objects; those objects, as being supernatural, when
not represented to our senses by material symbols, must
be set before the mind in propositions. The formula,
which embodies a dogma for the theologian, readily
suggests an object for the worshipper.[12]

We have come a long way from *The Arians*, where dogma
was seen as hardly more than a necessary evil, to a position
where doctrinal formulations are viewed as indispensable
for personal faith. It is not just that dogma protects religion
from error, but doctrinal propositions are now viewed as
integral to faith itself, which can hardly exist without some
knowledge of what it seeks to worship. Of course, Newman
knew when he wrote *The Arians* that the believer cannot
worship Christ without knowing something of his divinity;
but he seemed to have thought that it was a pity Christianity
could not rest in the simplest kind of proclamation of faith,
without any dogmatic developments at all. Thirty-seven years
later, he is anxious both to explain and to refute this attitude.
Newman's final position is that far from there necessarily
being an opposition between a personal and a propositional
religion, the two should be mutually interdependent.

But because dogmatic propositions are implied by an
objective religion does not mean that it is possible, or even
desirable, to list all the doctrines which a Catholic at any
given time has to believe. The Church, Newman pointed
out, 'would be misrepresenting the real character of the
dispensation' and 'abdicating her function' by transferring
the faith of Catholics 'from resting on herself as the organ
of revelation . . . simply to a code of certain definite articles
or a written creed'.[13] The Catholic position is that 'the object
of faith is *not* simply certain articles . . . contained in the
dumb documents, but the whole word of God, explicit and

implicit, as dispensed by His living Church'.[14] A Catholic
cannot itemize the contents of revelation, since

> there are many things which we know on the whole,
> but of which we cannot tell the boundaries. I know what
> is morally right, yet I cannot draw a sharp line in matters
> of detail between what is right and what is wrong. And
> so there may be points in Revelation which do not
> positively and undeniably command my faith, while yet
> there are points which certainly do.

Newman uses a striking secular analogy to describe the
Church as the expounder and interpreter of revelation: it is
like 'a standing Apostolic committee – to answer questions,
which the Apostles are not here to answer, concerning what
they received and preached'. But because 'the Church does
not know more than the Apostles knew, there are many
questions which the Church cannot answer'.[15] The Church,
however, has to be infallible since Christianity 'is no mere
philosophy thrown upon the world at large, no mere quality
of mind and thought, no mere beautiful and deep sentiment
or subjective opinion, but a substantive message from above,
guarded and preserved in a visible polity'. It was because
God 'willed the Gospel to be a revelation acknowledged and
authenticated, to be public, fixed, and permanent', that 'He
framed a Society of men to be its home, its instrument, and
its guarantee', so that the 'rulers of that Association are the
legal trustees, so to say, of the sacred truths which He spoke
to the Apostles by word of mouth'.[16]

It is, then, ultimately not to codified doctrines but to the
living communion of persons that is the Church to which
Catholics must look for the Christian revelation, which in
fact is the revelation of Christ. Nor is Catholicism equivalent
to its defined dogmas, since the Catholic faith cannot be
anything but the word of God. For all the necessity of doctrinal propositions, the Christian revelation is of a person and
is transmitted by a communion of persons who in turn are
passing on the message of God.

5

THE PERSONS OF THE TRINITY

Trinitarian theology in the West has traditionally started with the one divine substance, and then only secondarily moved on to the distinctions between the three persons of Father, Son, and Spirit. Or, in other words, it has begun from an abstraction rather than a person. The East, on the other hand, has always begun with the personal God who is the Father. The Father therefore has a Son who possesses consequently the same divine nature. The Father also has a Spirit who proceeds from the Father as Father, and so from the Father through the Son, possessing consequently the same divine nature as Father and Son by virtue of the procession. Thus Eastern theology concentrates on the different persons, beginning with the Father and then going on to the other persons who all possess the same divine nature. Unlike in Western theology, this divine nature is consequential rather than primary and the unity of the nature is the result of the procession of the persons.

In recent times a Catholic theologian like Karl Rahner has insisted on the importance of distinguishing the different functions of the three persons of the Trinity. In his own time Newman maintained the Eastern tradition. Pointing out that no problem was more acute for the early Christians than the apparent discrepancy between professing the oneness of God and belief in the Trinity, he wrote:

> Christianity began its teaching by denouncing poly-
> theism as wicked and absurd; but the retort on the part
> of the polytheist was obvious:– Christianity taught a
> Divine Trinity: how was this consistent with its profession

of a Monarchy? . . . Catholic theologians met this difficulty, both before and after the Nicene Council, by
insisting on the unity of origin, which they taught as
existing in the Divine Triad, the Son and Spirit having a
communicated divinity from the Father, and a personal
unity with Him . . . It was for the same reason that the
Father was called God absolutely, while the Second and
Third Persons were designated by Their personal names
of 'the Son', or 'the Word', and 'the Holy Ghost'; viz.
because they are to be regarded, not as separated from,
but as inherent in the Father.

Rather than the divine nature taking precedence over the
persons of the Trinity, the divine nature was seen by the
Greek Fathers as existing first of all in God the Father:
'instead of saying "Father, Son and Spirit, are one substance
(unum)", they would say "In one God and Father are the
Son and Spirit"; the words "One Father" standing not only
for the Person of the Father, but connecting that sole Divine
Substance which is one with His Person'.

This doctrine of the primacy of the Father was played
down in the West because of its abuse by the Arians who
questioned the divinity of Christ. But Newman was clear that
'what St. Irenaeus, St. Athanasius, and St. Basil taught, can
never be put aside. It is as true now as when those great
Fathers enunciated it; and if true, it cannot be ignored
without some detriment to the fullness and symmetry of the
Catholic dogma'. It is, he thought, of particular importance
in understanding the incarnation:

> One obvious use of it is to facilitate to the imagination
> the descent of the Divine Nature to the human, as
> revealed in the doctrine of the Incarnation; the Eternal
> Son of God becoming by a second birth the Son of God
> in time, is a line of thought which preserves to us the
> continuity of idea in the Divine Revelation; whereas, if
> we say abruptly that the Supreme Being became the
> Son of Mary, this, however true when taken by itself,
> still by reason of the infinite distance between God and
> man, acts in the direction of the Nestorian error of a

Christ with two Persons, as certainly as the doctrine of the *Principatus*, when taken by itself, favours the Arian error of a merely human Christ.[1]

Newman also thought it is better to say that the Son of God rather than simply God became man, as it was by no means arbitrary that the Son rather than the Father became incarnate: in fact the persons of the Trinity have different functions and roles:

> our Lord's Sonship is not only the guarantee to us of His Godhead, but also the condition of His incarnation. As the Son was God, so on the other hand was the Son suitably made man; it belonged to Him to have the Father's perfections, it became Him to assume a servant's form. We must beware of supposing that the Persons of the Ever-blessed and All-holy Trinity differ from each other only in this, that the Father is not the Son, and the Son is not the Father. They differ in this besides, that the Father *is* the Father, and the Son *is* the Son. While They are one in substance, Each has distinct characteristics which the Other has not. Surely those sacred Names have a meaning in them, and must not lightly be passed over.[2]

Nor is the incarnation simply a temporary state the Son takes on in order to achieve our redemption. For he does not cease to be the incarnate Word after the end of his earthly life. Rather it is the same incarnate, albeit now glorified, Son who continues his mediatorial intercession for humankind in heaven as the new head of the human race. For if through the incarnation human nature was renewed in Christ, 'glorious and wonderful beyond our thoughts', as a result of the resurrection that same nature was raised up in glory, so that 'Henceforth, we dare aspire to enter into the heaven of heavens, and to live for ever in God's presence, because the first-fruits of our race are already there in the Person of His Only-begotten Son'.[3] The bodily resurrection is essential, otherwise Christ in effect leaves part of the human nature he took to himself on earth in the shape of a discarded body and achieves only a partial resurrection in the spirit. Following the Eastern rather than the Western tradition, Newman insists that the resurrection is a logical consequence of the incarnation: 'Corruption had no power over that Sacred Body, the fruit of a miraculous conception.' When Christ was raised from the dead, 'the Divine Essence streamed forth (so to say) on every side, and environed His Manhood, as in a cloud of glory. So transfigured was His Sacred Body, that He who had deigned to be born of a woman, and to hang upon the cross, had subtle virtue in Him, like a spirit, to pass through the closed doors to His assembled followers.'[4] But if the resurrection completes, as it were, the incarnation, it also leads on directly to the ascension, for when Christ was raised from the dead, he was at the same time raised up in glory to the Father. It was necessary that the post-resurrection appearances should cease and that Christ should leave this world in order that we might receive the Holy Spirit, not as a kind of compensation or consolation, as so many Christians tend to assume, for the departure of Christ, but as the person of the Trinity who makes Christ even more personally and really present to Christians than was possible during his earthly ministry: 'We are able to see that the Saviour, when once He entered into this world, never so departed as to suffer things to be as they were before He came; for He is still with us, not in mere gifts, but by the substitution of His Spirit for Himself, and that, both in the Church, and in the souls of individual Christians.'[5] For it was Pentecost that applied the resurrection to our human situation by making the risen and glorified Christ savingly present in each individual Christian as well as the Church through the Holy Spirit. 'Christ's bodily presence, which was limited to place', had to be 'exchanged for the manifold spiritual indwelling of the Comforter within us'.[6] The Son returned to the Father, and in his place came 'the Eternal Love whereby the Father and the Son have dwelt in each other', the Holy Spirit, the third person of the Trinity. Newman insists that 'the Holy Ghost's coming is so really His coming, that we might as well say that He was not here in the days of His flesh, when He was visibly in the world, as deny that He is here now, when He is here by His Divine Spirit'.[7] This new presence was necessary, because 'the Spirit came to finish in us, what Christ had finished in Himself, but left unfinished as regards us. To Him it is committed to apply to us severally all that Christ had done for us'. Through the Spirit, Christ's redemption comes to each one of us: 'What was actually done by Christ in the flesh eighteen hundred years ago, is in type and resemblance really wrought in us one by one even to the end of time.'[8]

There are two points, then, that Newman is making to show that the coming of the Holy Spirit is absolutely integral to our redemption. In both cases the gift is a personal one. First, it makes it possible for Christ to be omnipresent in the most intimately personal way as it was not possible for him in a bodily form. Second, the gift of the Spirit brings home Christ's redemption personally to each individual. For through the Spirit we experience all the salvific acts and experiences of Christ, as Newman declares in a magnificent passage which is worth quoting at length:

> He was born of the Spirit, and we too are born of the Spirit. He was justified by the Spirit, and so are we. He was pronounced the well-beloved Son, when the Holy Ghost descended on Him; and we too cry Abba, Father, through the Spirit sent into our hearts. He was led into the wilderness by the Spirit; He did great works by the Spirit; He offered himself to death by the Eternal Spirit; He was raised from the dead by the Spirit; He was declared to be the Son of God by the Spirit of holiness on His resurrection: we too are led by the same Spirit into and through this world's temptations; we, too, do our works of obedience by the Spirit; we die from sin, we rise again unto righteousness through the Spirit; and we are declared to be God's sons, – declared, pronounced, dealt with as righteous, – through our resurrection unto holiness in the Spirit.

But this appropriation of the dispensation of Christ by the power of the Spirit may also be seen as Christ's own personal action, since the Spirit does not render the Son redundant by replacing him but rather makes him present by substituting for him. Thus we could put it in another way by ascribing the same acts and works to Christ himself rather than the Spirit:

> Christ Himself vouchsafes to repeat in each of us in figure and mystery all that He did and suffered in the flesh. He is formed in us, born in us, suffers in us, rises again in us, lives in us; and this not by a succession of events, but all at once: for He comes to us as a Spirit, all dying, all rising again, all living.[9]

But this substitution is no pale reflection of the reality, for Christ is now more deeply and really present through the Spirit than he could ever be in the flesh: the 'intercourse' we can now have with him is 'more high and gracious' and also 'more awful' than any the Apostles enjoyed during his early life.

> When He had once ascended, henceforth for unstudied speech there were solemn rites; for familiar attendance there were mysterious ministerings; for questioning at will there was silent obedience; for sitting at table there was bowing in adoration; for eating and drinking there was fasting and watching . . . Such was the vision of the glorified Saviour of man, returning to His redeemed in the power of the Spirit, with a Presence more pervading because more intimate, and more real because more hidden.[10]

The Spirit is no general abstraction or impersonal force but the third person of the Trinity with whom the Son is indissolubly united and through whom Christ can enter the hearts of all the baptized in a way that was impossible before. For where the Spirit is there necessarily is the Son too, since the Spirit does not replace the Son:

> Let us not for a moment suppose that God the Holy Ghost comes in such sense that God the Son remains away. No; He has not so come that Christ does not come, but rather He comes that Christ may come in

His coming. Through the Holy Ghost we have communion with Father and Son . . . The Holy Spirit causes,
faith welcomes, the indwelling of Christ in the heart.
Thus the Spirit does not take the place of Christ in the
soul, but secures that place to Christ.

And through the indwelling of the Holy Spirit, which assures
us of Christ's presence, we are also united to the Father, 'for
He who once was on earth, has now departed from this
visible scene of things in a mysterious, twofold way, both to
His Father and into our hearts, thus making the Creator
and His creatures one'.[11]

Like the Greek Fathers, Newman sees justification not in
terms of an *act* of faith or of works, but in terms of the
person of the Spirit through whose indwelling the Christian
is deified or divinized. This personal union is very different
from the abstract Western idea of grace as negatively a
remedy for sin and as a mere quality of the soul. For
Newman it is Christ himself through the Spirit who justifies
us, as he makes clear at the end of that great passage on the
work of the Holy Spirit already quoted:

His [Christ's] whole economy in all its parts is ever in
us all at once; and this divine presence constitutes the
title of each of us to heaven; that is what He will
acknowledge and accept at the last day. He will acknowledge Himself, – His image in us, – as though we
reflected Him, and He, on looking round about, dis-
cerned at once who were His; those, namely, who gave
back to Him His image. He impresses us with the seal
of the Spirit, in order to avouch that we are His. As
the King's image appropriates the coin to him, so the
likeness of Christ in us separates us from the world and
assigns us over to the kingdom of heaven.[12]

This justifying presence of Christ in the believer comes
through the indwelling of the Holy Spirit – 'He pervades
us . . . as light pervades a building, or as a sweet perfume
the folds of some honourable robe; so that, in Scripture
language, we are said to be in Him, and He in us.' For the

indwelling of the Spirit necessarily involves the presence of the other two persons of the Trinity as well: 'we are assured of some real though mystical fellowship with the Father, Son, and Holy Spirit... so that... by a real presence in the soul... God is one with every believer, as in a consecrated Temple.'[13]

To be justified, then, is not simply to be counted righteous, as Protestants were supposed to hold, but to be made righteous from within by God – 'not a change merely in God's dealings towards us, like the pale and wan sunshine of a winter's day, but... the possession of Himself.'[14] It was essentially a change wrought internally, not externally. After all, it was

> the great promise of the Gospel, that the Lord of all, who had hitherto manifested Himself externally to His servants, should take up His abode in their hearts... Though He had come in our flesh, so as to be seen and handled, even this was not enough. Still he was external and separate; but after His ascension He descended again by and in His Spirit, and then at length the promise was fulfilled.[15]

Redemption was not complete with Christ's death on the cross, nor is justification simply the victory of calvary imputed to us. Salvation would be incomplete without Pentecost, when the 'dreadful reality' of original sin was overcome by a 'new righteousness', a 'real righteousness' which 'comes from the Holy and divine Spirit', so that 'our works, done in the Spirit of Christ, have a justifying *principle* in them, and that is the presence of the All-holy Spirit', which 'hallows those acts, that life, that obedience of which it is the original cause, and which it orders and fashions'.[16] Justification, therefore, is a profoundly personal reality, since, just as 'the presence of a soul is the mode in which God gives man life, so the presence of the Holy Spirit is the mode in which God gives him righteousness'.[17] As a result of by-passing the Reformation controversy over whether we are justified by faith or by works, a dispute which presupposed a late medieval scholastic theology of grace that had lost touch with the sources in Scripture and the Fathers, Newman can propose a radical solution which is none other than the rediscovery of the great Johannine and Pauline doctrine of the personal indwelling of the Holy Spirit in the individual believer: 'the presence of the Holy Ghost shed abroad in our hearts, the Author both of faith and of renewal, this is really that which makes us righteous, and . . . our righteousness is the possession of that presence.' Justification, then, 'is wrought by the power of the Spirit, or rather by His presence within us', while 'faith and renewal are both present also, but as fruits of it'. The 'great gift' of justification is not a merely abstract 'supernatural quality imparted to the soul by God's grace', as Western scholasticism held, but a personal presence, 'the indwelling of Christ' through the Holy Spirit 'in the Christian soul'.[18]

We have seen how Newman's view of the human person leads him to postulate the existence of a personal God as the key to the meaning and nature of the person. This personal God who is ultimately the only fulfilment of the human person finds unique concrete embodiment and realization in the incarnation of Christ. But, as we have now shown, the person of Christ is not merely a historical figure, essentially detached from the existence of man, but is more personally and more really an intimate part of the Christian's life than he ever was to those among whom he lived out his earthly life. We must now turn to consider how the believer receives the gift of the Holy Spirit, which also makes possible the indwelling of the other two persons of the Trinity, and which for Newman constitutes the heart and reality of the Christian life. For grace is not merely a quality in the soul, but is essentially God's gift of himself. Indeed, in the famous chorus 'Praise to the Holiest in the Height' from *The Dream of Gerontius* (1865), Newman actually calls God's ultimate self-giving in the incarnation 'a higher gift than grace', namely, 'God's Presence and His very Self,/And Essence all-divine'.[19]

6

CHRIST'S PERSONAL PRESENCE IN THE SACRAMENTS

The late Charles Stephen Dessain, the founder of modern Newman studies, once wrote that, for Newman, 'True Christianity is the presence of Persons.'[1] This is as true of Newman's idea of the sacraments as of his approach to the existence of God.

Newman's conception of sacramentality again reflects the influence of the early Fathers, who start, as we have seen, from a very high view of the incarnation as the divinization of human flesh. Consequently, our own personal divinization has also to be achieved in an incarnational way through visible symbols.[2] So that we can share in the deification of human nature which his incarnation made possible, Christ comes *personally* to each of us individually, and the way he does this is through the sacraments: 'Our Lord, by becoming man, has found a way whereby to sanctify that nature, of which His own manhood is the pattern specimen. He inhabits us personally, and His inhabitation is effected by the channel of the Sacraments.' Through 'His indwelling', Christ is the 'immediate' source of 'spiritual life to each of His elect individually'.[3]

The divine indwelling is effected first by baptism which is the primary sacrament because through it the Christian receives the gift of the Holy Spirit. In a sermon based on a text from St Paul's first letter to the Corinthians, 'By one Spirit are we all baptized into one body', Newman explains:

As there is One Holy Ghost, so there is one only visible
Body of Christians . . . and one Baptism which admits
men into it. This is implied in the text . . . But more
than this is taught us in it; not only that the Holy Ghost
is in the Church, and that Baptism admits into it, but
that the Holy Ghost admits by means of Baptism, that
the Holy Ghost baptizes; in other words, that each individual member receives the gift of the Holy Ghost as a
preliminary step, a condition, or a means of his being
incorporated into the Church; or, in our Saviour's
words, that no one can enter, except to be regenerated
in order to enter it.[4]

While, then, we cannot receive the sacrament of baptism in
any individualistic kind of way but only from the Church,
nevertheless the Church can only bestow baptism because,
as Newman says, 'the Holy Ghost is in the Church'. That is
to say, the gift of baptism is the personal act of the Holy
Spirit – 'the Holy Ghost baptizes,' Newman insists: 'Baptism
is an instrument of the Holy Ghost.'[5] And this gift is not a
general gift which the Church passes on to us collectively, for
it is 'each individual member' of the Church who personally
receives the gift. The indwelling of the Holy Spirit, then,
can only come about in the Christian through baptism.
Nothing is visible, but 'the Spirit of God is come into, and
dwells in the child baptized'.[6]

There is another reason, apart from the fundamentally
incarnational nature of Christianity, why sacraments are so
important. And that is, Newman thought, because the Christian religion 'is of a personal nature, and implies the
acknowledgement of a particular Providence, of a God
speaking, not merely to the world at large, but to this person
or that, to one and not to another'. The Bible, on the other
hand, 'is a common possession, and speaks to one man as
much and as little as to his neighbour', but human nature
'requires something special', something of a highly personal
character.[7] This, then, is partly why we have sacraments, so
that Christ can come to each of us individually and personally. This, of course, is not intended to suggest that Newman

neglected the larger dimension of the Church, the body of Christ, the people of God, the communal or social character of Catholic Christianity which until the Second Vatican Council had been so ignored and neglected.[8] The Holy Spirit can only baptize by means of the Church, which at the same time is the communion of all those baptized in the Spirit: 'All must receive their Baptism from Christians already baptized, and they in their turn must have received the Sacrament from former Christians, themselves already incorporated in a body then previously existing.'[9]

In one of the finest passages in the *Parochial and Plain Sermons*, there is a marvellous evocation of the mystery of the sacraments, which are seen as supremely personal, but elusive, encounters with the Christ whose incarnation demands a continuing incarnational presence in the form of material symbols:

> In these is manifested in greater or less degree, according to the measure of each, that Incarnate Saviour, who is one day to be our Judge, and who is enabling us to bear His presence then, by imparting it to us in measure now. A thick black veil is spread between this world and the next. We mortal men range up and down it, to and fro, and see nothing. There is no access through it into the next world. In the Gospel this veil is not removed; it remains, but every now and then marvellous disclosures are made to us of what is behind it. At times we seem to catch a glimpse of a Form which we shall hereafter see face to face. We approach, and in spite of the darkness, our hands, or our head, or our brow, or our lips become, as it was, sensible of the contact of something more than earthly. We know not where we are, but we have been bathing in water, and a voice tells us that it is blood. Or we have a mark signed upon our foreheads, and it spake of Calvary. Or we recollect a hand laid upon our heads, and surely it had the print of nails in it, and resembled Him who with a touch gave sight to the blind and raised the dead. Or we have been eating and drinking; and it was not a dream surely, that

> One fed us from His wounded side, and renewed our
> nature by the heavenly meat He gave. Thus in many
> ways He, who is Judge to us, prepares us to be judged,
> – He, who is to glorify us, prepares us to be glorified,
> that He may not take us unawares; but that when the
> voice of the Archangel sounds, and we are called to
> meet the Bridegroom, we may be ready.[10]

It is important to notice that although the magical prose
powerfully suggests the numinous and unearthly, there is
also a very strong sense of a personal, albeit hidden, presence. We feel in the realm of the spiritual and supernatural,
but we are not merely confronted by impersonal forces.
Behind the veil that separates this world from the next,
there is not something but someone, and someone who is
not only 'Judge' but also 'Bridegroom'.

It is not surprising that Newman sees the real presence in
the Eucharist as above all the *personal* presence of Christ.
After all, a theology of the real presence or transubstan-
tiation, according to which Christ's body and blood become
really or substantially present in the elements or species of
bread and wine, may only support in effect a rather impersonal spirituality. But Newman's eucharistic spirituality centres not so much on the body and blood as on the *person* to
whom they belong. Thus Newman concludes a sermon on
the Eucharist with the conclusion that Christians there
experience 'the foretaste of heaven' since there especially
they 'seek Him in invisible Presence, whom they shall here-
after see face to face'.[11] Once again, we return to what for
Newman is really the fundamental doctrine of Christianity,
the incarnation.

> No one realizes the Mystery of the Incarnation but must
> feel disposed towards that of Holy Communion. Let us
> pray Him to give us an earnest longing after Him – a
> thirst for His Presence – an anxiety to find Him – a joy
> on hearing that He is to be found, even now, under the
> veil of sensible things, – and a good hope that *we* shall
> find Him there.[12]

In a beautiful ending to another of the *Parochial and Plain Sermons*, Newman imagines recollecting in the future the emotion attached to the celebration of early communion services in the Anglican Church:

> ... how pleasant to come, day after day, quietly and calmly, to kneel before our Maker, – week after week, to meet our Lord and Saviour. How soothing will then be the remembrance of His past gifts! we shall remember how we got up early in the morning, and how all things, light or darkness, sun or air, cold or freshness, breathed of Him, – of Him, the Lord of glory, who stood over us, and came down upon us, and gave Himself to us, and poured forth milk and honey for our sustenance, though we saw Him not. Surely we have all, and abound: we are full.[13]

Through receiving Holy Communion, we not only meet Christ personally but we actually become Christ, for as a result of eating his body and drinking his blood he enters into and becomes one with us:

> We eat the sacred bread, and our bodies become sacred; they are not ours; they are Christ's; they are instinct with that flesh which saw not corruption; they are inhabited by His Spirit; they become immortal; they die but to appearance, and for a time; they spring up when their sleep is ended, and reign with Him for ever.[14]

But, as we have seen, Newman's emphasis really falls not so much on Christ's body and blood becoming really present in the consecrated bread and wine as on the very person of Christ becoming present in the sacrament:

> He who is at the right hand of God, manifests Himself in that Holy Sacrament as really and fully as if He were visibly there ... Such is the glorious presence which faith sees in the Holy Communion, though every thing looks as usual to the natural man. Not gold or precious stones, pearls of great price or gold of Ophir, are to the eye of faith so radiant as those lowly elements which

He, the Highest, is pleased to make the means of conveying to our hearts and bodies His own gracious self.[15]

The 'real presence', Newman insists, is not a vague metaphor, but the reason why the Eucharist is 'the greatest and highest of all the Sacramental mysteries' is because:

> Christ, who died and rose again for us, is in it spiritually present, in the fulness of His death and of His resurrection. We call His presence in this Holy Sacrament a spiritual presence, not as if 'spiritual' were but a name or mode of speech, and He were really absent, but by way of expressing that He who is present there can neither be seen nor heard; that He cannot be approached or ascertained by any of the senses; that He is not present in place, that He is not present carnally, though He is really present.[16]

If as an Anglican Newman saw the Eucharist as 'a continual revelation of the Incarnation',[17] when he became a Catholic his great discovery was of the continuation of the Eucharist in the reservation of the sacrament – 'a Presence in the sacred Tabernacle, not as a form of words, or as a notion, but as an Object as real as we are real'.[18] It is strange that he seems to have known nothing about this universal Catholic practice, but he had been careful to keep his distance before his conversion.

> We went over not realizing those privileges which we have found *by* going . . . I could not have fancied the extreme, ineffable comfort of being in the same house with Him who cured the sick and taught His disciples . . . When I have been in Churches abroad, I have religiously abstained from acts of worship, though it was a most soothing comfort to go into them – nor did I know what was going on . . . I did not know, or did not observe, the tabernacle Lamp – but now after tasting of the awful delight of worshipping God in His Temple, how unspeakably cold is the idea of a Temple without that Divine Presence! One is tempted to say what is the meaning, what is the use of it?[19]

This overpowering sense of the personal presence of Christ in Catholic chapels and churches is a constant theme in Newman's letters during the months after his conversion. It is not the ritual of the Church but the perpetual sacramental presence of Christ that fills his imagination in the early days of his new Catholic life: 'It is such an incomprehensible blessing to have Christ in bodily presence in one's house, within one's walls, as swallows up all other privileges . . . To know that He is close by – to be able again and again through the day to go in to Him.' Part of the attraction was certainly a very Newmanian one – namely, that it helped create 'the deep impression of religion as an objective fact'.[20] But the 'objective fact' was not a thing but the person of Christ abidingly present. Again and again he alluded to that 'Presence of our Undying Life, hidden but ever working', that was betokened by 'the distant glimmering Lamp'. From Italy, where he had gone to prepare for ordination to the priesthood, he wrote: 'It is really most wonderful to see the Divine Presence looking out almost into the open streets from the various Churches . . . I never knew what worship was, as an objective fact, till I entered the Catholic Church.' The Church's note of unity was supremely confirmed, it seemed to Newman, by this sacramental omnipresence of Christ himself: nothing, he declared, 'has brought home to me so much the Unity of the Church, as the presence of its Divine Founder and Life wherever I go – All places are, as it were, one.'[21] It is not surprising that when the hero of his novel *Loss and Gain* (1848) attends a Catholic church for the first time, it is not the beauty of the liturgy that impresses him as much as 'the Great Presence, which makes a Catholic Church different from every other place in the world'.[22] Just as the Eucharist, of course, is 'a continual revelation' not only of the incarnation but also of the crucifixion and resurrection, so too the reservation of the sacrament assures the presence of both the incarnate and the crucified and risen Christ, thus ensuring that 'the Atonement of Christ is not a thing at a distance, or like the sun standing over against us and separated off from us, but that we are surrounded by an *atmosphere* and are in a medium, through which his warmth and light flow in upon us on every side'.[23]

We have seen how Newman's understanding of the nature of the human person involves the existence of a personal God. The historical person of Jesus Christ is the unique revelation of this personal God. However, the person of Christ is not a distant person in history but is intimately present to every Christian in and through the Holy Spirit, the third person of the divine Trinity. This divine indwelling is effected in the individual believer through the sacrament of baptism first of all, but is continued sacramentally, especially through Christ's personal presence in the Eucharist. However, these sacraments are only possible through the Church, and so we must now turn to consider how Newman's personalism shapes his ecclesiology.

7

THE CHURCH A COMMUNION OF PERSONS

Newman's conception of the Church as primarily the communion of those who have received the Holy Spirit in baptism originates again in his study of the Eastern Fathers. It was very different from the usual institutional and juridical ecclesiology of the scholastic, Tridentine Catholicism of his time. As an Anglican, Newman taught that the Church 'is a visible body, invested with, or . . . existing in invisible privileges', for 'the Church would cease to be the Church, did the Holy Spirit leave it', since 'its outward rites and forms are nourished and animated by the living power which dwells within it'.[1] Indeed the Church is the Holy Spirit's 'especial dwelling-place'.[2] For while Christ came 'to die for us; the Spirit came to make us one in Him who had died and was alive, that is, to form the Church'. The Church, then, is 'the one mystical body of Christ . . . quickened by the Spirit' – and is 'one' by virtue of the Holy Spirit 'giving it *life*'.[3]

In the historic creeds Christians profess their belief in the oneness of the Church as an essential note like holiness, catholicity, and apostolicity. What Newman as an Anglican called 'Gospel privileges' were, he realized, intimately connected

> with the circumstance or condition of unity in those who receive them; the image of Christ and token of their acceptance being stamped upon them *then*, at that moment, when they are considered as *one*; so that

henceforth the whole multitude, no longer viewed as mere individual men, become portions or members of the indivisible Body of Christ Mystical, so knit together in Him by Divine Grace, that all have what He has, and each has what all have.[4]

Far from this unity being merely a matter of fraternal union, let alone institutional cohesion, it is in fact a oneness created by the personal presence of Christ in and through the person of the Spirit:

He who came for ever, came as a Spirit, and, so coming, did for His own that which the visible flesh and blood of the Son of man, from its very nature, could not do, viz., He came into the souls of all who believe, and taking possession of them, He, being One, knit them all together into one. Christ, by coming in the flesh, provided an external or apparent unity, such as had been under the Law. He formed His Apostles into a visible society; but when He came again in the Person of His Spirit, He made them all in a real sense one, not in name only. For they were no longer arranged merely in the form of unity, as the limbs of the dead may be, but they were parts and organs of one unseen power; they really depended upon, and were offshoots of that which was One; their separate persons were taken into a mysterious union with things unseen, were grafted upon and assimilated to the spiritual body of Christ, which is One, even by the Holy Ghost, in whom Christ has come again to us. Thus Christ came, not to make us one, but to die for us: the Spirit came to make us one in Him who had died and was alive, that is, to form the Church.[5]

Not only, then, do individuals become Christians and are justified by the gift of the Holy Spirit, but it is the Spirit who also binds together those individuals into the unity of the Church. But in both cases it is in fact Christ himself who comes personally in the Spirit.

If Newman sees the Church first and foremost in terms

of the mystery of the indwelling of the Holy Spirit, his subsequent ecclesiology is firmly grounded on this fundamental idea of the Church as the communion of individual persons baptized by the Spirit into the unity of Christ's body. His theology of the Church, then, is essentially personal rather than institutional, concrete rather than theoretical, practical rather than ideal. Now since even the most uncatholic forms of Christianity involve some kind of ecclesial fellowship, any Christian spirituality must address itself to the difficulties and problems inherently present in community life. But of no church, of course, is this more true than the Roman Catholic Church. And as Newman reflected on these problems during the latter half of the nineteenth century as the tide of papal ultramontanism rose even higher, he came more and more to believe that his old Anglican preconceptions about the corruptions of Rome in fact missed the point. This was not because there were no corruptions (although Newman changed his mind about the nature of these corruptions), but because he saw that the root cause was not solely of a theological character, but rather arose out of the complexity of life itself since the Church was neither merely an impersonal, juridical institution nor an abstract ideal but in fact was at the human level a communion consisting of many different kinds of individuals with different charisms and functions. A shared unity could not exclude the resulting tensions and even conflicts, any more than the Church, which is a living organism not an inanimate thing, can be free from the possibility of corruption. Because the Church is a communion of persons, we should not be surprised or alarmed by the stresses and strains and weaknesses of Catholicism. But it is a source of scandal to many inside and outside the Catholic Church, and therefore it is important to have a spirituality which takes account of the difficulty. Newman's personalistic ecclesiology offers a valuable approach to these problems.

In the historic creeds Christians profess their faith in One, Holy, Catholic, and Apostolic Church. And so the Church possesses what Newman once as an Anglican called 'the great Note of the Church', namely sanctity.[6] But if holiness

is an essential mark of the Church, then how is it that sin
seems also to be a distinctly marked characteristic as well?
The difficulty led Newman to develop a veritable theology
of the corruption of the Church, and indeed his thinking
on this subject was a central factor in his conversion to
Roman Catholicism. The first obvious point to make is that
'Even among the Apostles themselves, one was a "Devil" ':
'No wonder then that ever since, whether among the rulers
or the subjects of the Church, sin has abounded.'[7] But in a
much less dramatic way the Church in its sinful human
members cannot help but seem sinful, and more sinful than
holy:

> Even supposing there were a society of men influenced
> individually by Christian motives, still this society, viewed
> as a whole, would be a worldly one; I mean a society
> holding and maintaining many errors, and countenanc-
> ing many bad practices. Evil ever floats at the top. And
> if we inquire why it is that the good in Christians is seen
> less than the bad? I answer, first, because there is less of
> it; and secondly, because evil forces itself upon general
> notice, and good does not.

And so, Newman argues, there is an important sense in
which the real holiness of the Church is hidden from view:

> It is only the actions of others which we see for the
> most part . . . God only sees the circumstances under
> which a man acts, and why he acts in this way and not
> in that. God only sees perfectly the train of thought
> which preceded his action, the motive, and the
> reasons . . . Think for a moment, how many hours in
> the day every man is left wholly to himself and his God,
> or rather how few minutes he is in intercourse with
> others – consider this, and you will perceive how it is
> that the life of the Church is hid with God, and how it
> is that the outward conduct of the Church must neces-
> sarily look like the world, even far more than it really
> is like it.

There are words of warning against judging people by their

outward behaviour, which ought to make us more cautious in our criticisms of the Church, especially perhaps of its leaders:

> Consider, moreover, how much there is, while we are in the body, to stand in the way of one mind communicating with another. We are imprisoned in the body, and our intercourse is by means of words, which feebly represent our real feelings. Hence the best motives and truest opinions are misunderstood.[8]

However, genuine corruptions in the Church should be no surprise as they were clearly predicted by Christ himself in the gospels. In Newman's earlier Protestant years as an Anglican, he thought that such prophecies had been visibly fulfilled in the corruptions particularly of the papacy. Later, as a Catholic, he came to see these same corruptions not as evidence that the Church of Rome was the Church of the Antichrist but rather almost as notes of the true Church! For corruption is now seen as inseparable from a living communion of persons: 'Things that do not admit of abuse have very little life in them.'[9] And it is this very quality of 'life' which Newman insists on as an especial note of the Church: 'The Church is emphatically a living body ... she alone revives even if she declines; heretical and schismatical bodies cannot keep life.'[10]

Not only did Christ predict scandals, but in the parable of the tares and the wheat, for example, he spoke of the Church 'as in its very constitution made up of good and bad'. The corruption of the Church has existed from the time of Judas Iscariot and indeed is so 'bound up with the very idea of Christianity' as to be 'almost a dogma'.[11] Given that the world is sinful, once 'it has poured into the Church, it has insulted and blasphemed the religion which it professed, in a special way, in which heathenism cannot insult it'. One would expect, Newman adds, to find greater corruption in the Catholic Church than in a Protestant Church, for 'a Protestant world cannot commit that sin which a Catholic world can'. When ordinary human weaknesses are 'coupled with that intense absolute faith which

Catholics have, and Protestants have not', one finds 'acts of inconsistency, of superstition, violence etc. which are not to be looked for external to the Catholic Church'.[12] In other words, on the old principle that the corruption of the best is the worst, if the claims of the Catholic Church are anything to go by, one would expect to find in it the greatest scandals. In particular, in regard to the papacy, 'where you have power, you will have the abuse of power – and the more absolute, the stronger, the more sacred the power, the greater and more certain will be its abuse'.[13] Because, too, the Church is a visible polity, it is also 'necessarily a political power, and to touch politics is to touch pitch'.[14]

Towards the end of his life, in the great 1877 Preface to the *Via Media*, Newman tackled the sensitive problem of corruption in a more profoundly theological manner. His starting-point are the three offices of Christ, which are shared by the Church, although they are exercised by a variety of members of the Church. The Church, he points out, is the mystical body of Christ, who 'is Prophet, Priest, and King; and after His pattern, and in human measure, Holy Church has a triple office too; not the Prophetical alone and in isolation . . . but three offices, which are indivisible, though diverse, viz. teaching, rule, and sacred ministry'. It follows that Christianity

> is at once a philosophy, a political power, and a religious rite: as a religion, it is Holy; as a philosophy, it is Apostolic; as a political power, it is imperial, that is, One and Catholic. As a religion, its special centre of action is pastor and flock; as a philosophy, the Schools; as a rule, the Papacy and its Curia.

These three different offices are based on different principles, use different means, and are liable to different corruptions:

> Truth is the guiding principle of theology and theological inquiries; devotion and edification, of worship; and of government, expedience. The instrument of theology is reasoning; of worship, our emotional nature; of rule,

command and coercion. Further, in man as he is, reasoning tends to rationalism; devotion to superstition and enthusiasm; and power to ambition and tyranny.

The difficulty of combining all three offices is well illustrated by the question, 'What line of conduct, except on the long, the very long run, is at once edifying, expedient, and true?' Certainly, the charism of infallibility protects the Catholic Church from error not only directly in teaching but also 'indirectly' in 'worship and political action also'; however, 'nothing but the gift of impeccability granted to her authorities would secure them from all liability to mistake in their conduct, policy, words and decisions'. The problem of exercising these three very different functions 'supplies the staple of those energetic charges and vivid pictures of the inconsistency, double-dealing, and deceit of the Church of Rome'.

Far from blaming the corruptions to be found in the Church on Catholic theology, as he had done as an Anglican, he now observes that 'ambition, craft, cruelty, and superstition are not commonly the characteristic of theologians', whereas the alleged corruptions in fact 'bear on their face the marks of having a popular or a political origin', and 'theology, so far from encouraging them, has restrained and corrected such extravagances as have been committed, through human infirmity, in the exercise of the regal and sacerdotal powers'. Indeed, he adds dramatically, religion is never 'in greater trouble than when, in consequence of national or international troubles, the Schools of theology have been broken up and ceased to be'. And he insists on the vital role of theologians:

> I say, then, Theology is the fundamental and regulating principle of the whole Church system. It is commensurate with Revelation, and Revelation is the initial and essential idea of Christianity. It is the subject-matter, the formal cause, the expression, of the Prophetical Office, and, as being such, has created both the Regal Office and the Sacerdotal. And it has in a certain sense a power of jurisdiction over those offices, as being its

own creations, theologians being ever in request and in employment in keeping within bounds both the political and popular elements in the Church's constitution, – elements which are far more congenial than itself to the human mind, are far more liable to excess and corruption . . . [15]

A charge often levelled at the Catholic Church is that of the corruption of its worship, in other words of superstition. But Newman argues that the kind of popular religion likely to cause scandal may be traced to the gospel itself, and he cites the example of the woman with the haemorrhage who hoped to be cured by touching the cloak of Jesus, who 'passed over the superstitious act' and healed her because of her faith. In fact, he praised her for 'what might, not without reason, be called an idolatrous act'. Actually the gospels show that the 'idolatry of ignorance' is not regarded on a level with other idolatries (of wealth, for example), which, however, are not normally 'shocking to educated minds'. Jesus constantly insisted on the necessity of faith – 'but where does He insist on the danger of superstition?' However, the fact remains that this and other incidents in the gospels 'form an aspect of Apostolic Christianity very different from that presented' by the Epistles of St Paul. 'Need men wait for the Medieval Church in order to make their complaint that the theology of Christianity does not accord with its religious manifestations?' Does 'a poor Neapolitan crone, who chatters to the crucifix' do anything inherently more superstitious than the woman with the haemorrhage? Given 'the ethical intelligence of the world at large', Newman would wonder 'whether that nation really had the faith, which is free in all its ranks and classes from all kinds and degrees of what is commonly considered superstition'.

There is no reason to be surprised if the Catholic Church, in the face of popular religion, finds it difficult 'to make her Sacerdotal office keep step with her Prophetical'. This applies obviously to the cult of the angels and saints, which, 'though ever to be watched with jealousy by theologians, because of human infirmity and perverseness ... has a normal place in revealed Religion'. For monotheism implies beings who are inferior to God but superior to human beings, and who are able to bridge 'the vast gulf which separates Him from man'. And so polytheism is only 'a natural sentiment corrupted'. The Church's mission is not 'to oppose herself to impulses' that are 'both natural and legitimate', though previously 'the instruments of sin, but to do her best, by a right use, to moderate and purify them'. The fact that the Church has not always been successful simply shows that 'there will ever be a marked contrariety between the professions of her theology and the ways and doings of a Catholic country'.[16]

Apart from corruption, the other problem that troubles many people is the alleged authoritarianism of the Catholic Church. Again, Newman's approach is not to attempt to work out an abstract or ideal theory that might apply to an impersonal institution. Instead he develops a theological view of the personal interaction of theologians and church authorities. In fact he sees this interaction in terms of a creative conflict. On the one hand are the duties of popes and bishops, and on the other hand the rights of theologians. Both parties are integral to the life of the Church, but their roles cannot be exactly demarcated since we are talking not about functionaries but about concrete persons with an individuality and life of their own.

On the one hand, Newman stresses the authority of the successors of the Apostles as 'a supereminent prodigious power sent upon earth to encounter and master a giant evil', both 'viewed in its fulness' and 'viewed in the concrete, as clothed and surrounded by the appendages of its high sovereignty'. Although infallibility strictly only belongs to solemn dogmatic definitions, Newman professes to submit not only to the traditions of the Church, but also 'to those other decisions of the Holy See, theological or not ... which, waiving the question of their infallibility, on the lowest ground come to me with a claim to be accepted and obeyed'. Nor does he feel any 'temptation at all to break in pieces the great legacy of thought' which the Church has inherited from its greatest thinkers. This raises the obvious objection that 'the restless intellect of our common humanity is utterly weighed down' by such an authority, 'so that, if this is to be the mode of bringing it into order, it is brought into order only to be destroyed'. Newman's reply is that in fact the 'energy of the human intellect . . . thrives and is joyous, with a tough elastic strength, under the terrible blows of the divinely-fashioned weapon, and is never so much itself as when it has lately been overthrown'. And he argues that far from being mutually contradictory, authority and reason need each other precisely because, paradoxically, each is actually sustained by conflict with the other:

> It is the vast Catholic body itself, and it only, which affords an arena for both combatants in that awful, never-dying duel. It is necessary for the very life of religion . . . that the warfare should be incessantly carried on. Every exercise of Infallibility is brought out into act by an intense and varied operation of the Reason, both as its ally and as its opponent, and provokes again, when it has done its work, a re-action of Reason against it; and, as in a civil polity the State exists and endures by means of the rivalry and collision, the encroachments and defeats of its constituent parts, so in like manner Catholic Christendom is no simple exhibition of religious absolutism, but presents a continuous picture of Authority and Private Judgment alternately advancing and retreating as the ebb and flow of the tide; – it is a vast assemblage of human beings with wilful intellects and wild passions, brought together into one by the beauty and the Majesty of a Superhuman Power, – into what may be called a large reformatory or training-school, not as if into a hospital or into a prison, not in order to be sent to bed, not to be buried alive, but (if I may change my metaphor) brought together as if into some moral factory, for the melting, refining, and moulding, by an incessant, noisy process, of the raw material of human nature, so excellent, so dangerous, so capable of divine purposes.[17]

It is obviously quite inappropriate to attempt to produce some kind of diagram of the relationship between the magisterium and theology since what one is really talking about are not so much two functions in the Church as two groups of people with different duties and prerogatives, both of whom need each other in their complementary roles. The fact that there may be tension between the two is not a sign of contradiction nor should it disguise their very real interdependence.

The infallible authority, Newman insists, 'is a supply for a need, and it does not go beyond that need', for its purpose is 'not to enfeeble the freedom or vigour of human thought in religious speculation, but to resist and control its extravagance'. As well as freely admitting the wide powers enjoyed by ecclesiastical authority, Newman wants to emphasize both the narrow limits of infallibility in defining as explicit doctrine what is already implicit in revelation, and also its rare occurrence (normally by a 'Pope in Ecumenical Council'). But, more important, he recognizes what '*is* the great trial to the Reason', namely, that the church authorities claim jurisdiction over a wide area of 'secular matters which bear upon religion'. These disciplinary rather than doctrinal judgments are not, however, infallible; nevertheless, they claim obedience (but not faith). Again, 'because there is a gift of infallibility in the Catholic Church', it does not necessarily follow that 'the parties who are in possession of it are in all their proceedings infallible'. Indeed, 'I think history supplies us with instances in the Church, where legitimate power has been harshly used.' The unequivocal assertion of the Church's legitimate authority is thus sharply qualified by these reminders of its limits and restraints. But the apparent discrepancy is resolved by the consideration that it does not 'follow that the substance of the acts of the ruling power is not right and expedient, because its manner may have been faulty'. In fact, Newman remarks tartly, 'high authorities act by means of instruments', and 'we know how such instruments claim for themselves the mane of their principals, who thus get the credit of faults which really are not theirs'.[18]

It is characteristic of Newman to develop his argument

not through abstract theory but by addressing the concrete cases of actual historical persons. History shows how even individual Protestants 'have before now obeyed the royal command to abstain from certain theological questions'. Moreover, despite all abuses, Newman insists that the ecclesiastical authorities have been 'mainly in the right, and that those whom they were hard upon were mainly in the wrong'. For example, Origen 'was wrong' and 'his opponents were right'. And yet 'who can speak with patience of his enemy and the enemy of St John Chrysostom, that Theophilus, bishop of Alexandria? who can admire or revere Pope Vigilius?' The contradiction is resolved by a completely fresh perspective, at once enlightening and provocative:

> In reading ecclesiastical history, when I was an Anglican, it used to be forcibly brought home to me, how the initial error of what afterwards became heresy was the urging forward of some truth against the prohibition of authority at an unseasonable time. There is a time for every thing, and many a man desires a reformation of an abuse, or the fuller development of a doctrine, or the adoption of a particular policy, but forgets to ask himself whether the right time for it is come: and knowing that there is no one who will be doing any thing towards its accomplishment in his own lifetime unless he does it himself, he will not listen to the voice of authority, and he spoils a good work in his own century, in order that another man, as yet unborn, may not have the opportunity of bringing it happily to perfection in the next. He may seem to the world to be nothing else than a bold champion for the truth and a martyr to free opinion, when he is just one of those persons whom the competent authority ought to silence; and, though the case may not fall within that subject-matter in which that authority is infallible, or the formal conditions of the exercise of that gift may be wanting, it is clearly the duty of authority to act vigorously in the case.

This, Newman admits, will arouse criticism, especially 'if the ruling power happens in its proceedings to evince any defect of prudence or consideration'. Mindful, no doubt, of his own difficulties with liberal Catholics who disliked his insistence on obedience, Newman adds that 'all those who take the part of that ruling authority will be considered as time-servers, or indifferent to the cause of uprightness and truth'. But that is not the conclusion of the sentence. The surprise, or rather the sting, lies in the second half, directed not at the liberals, but at the Ultramontanes: 'while, on the other hand, the said authority may be accidentally supported by a violent ultra party, which exalts opinions into dogmas, and has it principally at heart to destroy every school of thought but its own.'[19]

The proof, Newman continues, that infallibility has not crushed intellectual freedom in the Church is that it is 'individuals, and not the Holy See, that have taken the initiative, and given the lead to the Catholic mind, in theological inquiry'. 'Indeed,' he points out, 'it is one of the reproaches against the Roman Church, that it has originated nothing, and has only served as a sort of *remora* or break in the development of doctrine. And it is an objection which I really embrace as a truth; for such I conceive to be the main purpose of its extraordinary gift.'

The historical examples that follow are unrelentingly negative. The fact is that 'the Church of Rome possessed no great mind in the whole period of persecution'. There was not a single doctor till St Leo, who anyway taught only 'one point of doctrine'. Not even Pope St Gregory has a place in the history of theology. The greatest Western theologian, St Augustine, belonged, like the best early Latin theologians, to the African Church. Western theology, in fact, was formed to a considerable extent by heterodox theologians such as Tertullian and Origen and Eusebius, with the result that actual heretical 'questionings' became 'salutary truths'. Even ecumenical councils were guided by the 'individual reason' of a mere presbyter like Malchion, or a young deacon like Athanasius. At Trent too, particular theologians 'had a critical effect on some of the definitions of dogma'. The real, albeit hidden, conclusion is that history gives little support to the Ultramontane view of Rome as a kind of oracle of truth.

History too shows how little the authorities have interfered with the freedom of theologians. But Newman is not only protesting against the present by means of the past; he is also stating with great deliberateness his considered view on the crucial balance to be maintained between theology and the teaching authority of the Church. He begins by referring (provocatively) to that medieval theocratic society so idealized by many of his contemporaries:

> There never was a time when the intellect of the edu-cated class was more active, or rather more restless, than in the middle ages. And then again all through Church history from the first, how slow is authority in interfering! Perhaps a local teacher, or a doctor in some local school, hazards a proposition, and a controversy ensues. It smoulders or burns in one place, no one interposing; Rome simply lets it alone. Then it comes before a Bishop; or some priest, or some professor in some other seat of learning takes it up; and then there is a second stage of it. Then it comes before a University, and it may be condemned by the theological faculty. So the controversy proceeds year after year, and Rome is still silent. An appeal perhaps is next made to a seat of authority inferior to Rome; and then at last after a long while it comes before the supreme power. Meanwhile, the question has been ventilated and turned over and over again, and viewed on every side of it, and authority is called upon to pronounce a decision, which has already been arrived at by reason. But even then, per-haps the supreme authority hesitates to do so, and nothing is determined on the point for years; or so generally and vaguely, that the whole controversy has to be gone through again, before it is ultimately determined.

Newman refrains from outright criticism of the abuse of authority in the contemporary Church. But his point is clear enough.

It is manifest how a mode of proceeding, such as this, tends not only to the liberty, but to the courage, of the individual theologian or controversialist. Many a man has ideas, which he hopes are true, and useful for his day, but he is not confident about them, and wishes to have them discussed. He is willing, or rather would be thankful, to give them up, if they can be proved to be erroneous or dangerous, and by means of controversy he achieves his end. He is answered, and he yields; or on the contrary he finds that he is considered safe. He would not dare to do this, if he knew an authority, which was supreme and final, was watching every word he said, and made signs of assent or dissent to each sentence, as he uttered it. Then indeed he would be fighting, as the Persian soldiers, under the lash, and the freedom of his intellect might truly be said to be beaten out of him.

Nevertheless, he is ready to undermine his own indignation with the frank qualification that 'when controversies run high' then 'an interposition may ... advisably take place; and again, questions may be of that urgent nature, that an appeal must, as a matter of duty, be made at once to the highest authority in the Church'.

But the insistent emphasis on the universal character of the Church that follows barely conceals an unfavourable allusion to the Italian monopoly of the Holy See.

The multitude of nations which are within the fold of the Church will be found to have acted for its protection, against any narrowness, on the supposition of narrowness, in the various authorities at Rome, with whom lies the practical decision of controverted questions ... Then, again, such national influences have a providential effect in moderating the bias which the local influences of Italy may exert on the See of St Peter. It stands to reason that ... Rome must have in it an element of Italy; and it is no prejudice to the zeal and devotion with which we submit ourselves to the Holy See to admit

> this plainly . . . Catholicity is not only one of the notes
> of the Church, but . . . one of its securities.

And the conclusion is uncompromising:

> I trust that all European races will ever have a place in
> the Church, and assuredly I think that the loss of the
> English, not to say the German element, in its compo-
> sition has been a most serious misfortune. And certainly,
> if there is one consideration more than another which
> should make us English grateful to Pius the Ninth, it is
> that, by giving us a Church of our own, he has prepared
> the way for our own habits of mind, our own manner
> of reasoning, our own tastes, and our own virtues, find-
> ing a place and thereby a sanctification, in the Catholic
> Church.[20]

The Church, then, is not only a communion of persons, but
of persons who differ widely and constitute in their variety
part of the catholicity or wholeness of the Church.

Schematic, tidy blueprints find no place in Newman's
ecclesiology because the Church is a living community made
up of living people, with various gifts and talents and roles
to play, so that the Church's 'organization cannot be otherwise than complex, considering the many functions which
she has to fulfil'. Although the Church has always exercised
its three main offices,

> they were developed in their full proportions one after
> another, in a succession of centuries; first, in the primi-
> tive time it was recognized as a worship, springing up
> and spreading in the lower ranks of society . . . Then it
> seized upon the intellectual and cultivated class, and
> created a theology and schools of learning. Lastly it
> seated itself, as an ecclesiastical polity, among princes,
> and chose Rome for its centre.

The importance Newman attaches in the Preface to the
Via Media to theologians is significantly modified by important reservations: 'Yet theology cannot always have its own
way: it is too hard, too intellectual, too exact, to be always

equitable, or to be always compassionate.' Sometimes even a theologian in his writings has to 'let his devout nature betray itself between the joints of his theological harness'. Popular religion may, for example, reject a more accurate translation of the Bible because to 'the devotional mind what is new and strange is as repulsive, often as dangerous, as falsehood is to the scientific. Novelty is often error to those who are unprepared for it, from the refraction with which it enters into their conceptions.' However wrong the condemnation of Galileo,

> there was nothing wrong in censuring abrupt, startling, unsettling, unverified disclosures . . . at once uncalled for and inopportune, at a time when the limits of revealed truth had not as yet been ascertained. A man ought to be very sure of what he is saying, before he risks the chance of contradicting the word of God. It was safe, not dishonest, to be slow in accepting what nevertheless turned out to be true. Here is an instance in which the Church obliges Scripture expositors, at a given time or place, to be tender of the popular religious sense.

People's 'imaginations' have to become accustomed to religious changes, whereas 'when science crosses and breaks the received path of Revelation', religious people are criticized if 'they show hesitation to shift at a minute's warning their position, and to accept as truths shadowy views at variance with what they have ever been taught and have held'. The modern idea holds that it is 'a great moral virtue to be fearless and thorough in inquiry into facts', whereas the 'pursuit of truth in the subject-matter of religion . . . must always be accompanied by the fear of error'.[21] Elsewhere, Newman says:

> What the genius of the Church cannot bear is, changes in thought being hurried, abrupt, violent – out of tenderness to souls, for unlearned and narrow-minded men get unsettled and miserable. The great thing is to

move all together and then the change, as geological changes, must be very slow.

In a letter, however, Newman emphasizes the role of theology in preparing the Church for changes – 'it is the arena on which questions of development and change are argued out . . . it prepares the way, accustoming the mind of Catholics to the idea of the change'. Because theology also, he explains, 'protects' dogma by 'forming a large body of doctrine which must be got through before an attack can be made on the dogma', without theology 'the dogma of the Church would be the raw flesh without skin – nay or a tree without leaves – for, as devotional feelings clothe the dogma on the one hand, so does the teaching of [theology] on the other'.[22]

The Church allows much more freedom in devotion, which is 'of a subjective and personal nature', than in doctrine. This contrast is accentuated if 'ecclesiastical authority takes part with popular sentiment against a theological decision'. A very early example would be the occasion at Antioch when St Peter stopped associating with converts from paganism because of pressure from converts from Judaism, a lapse for which he was rebuked by St Paul. However, Paul himself was ready to conform to Jewish customs when necessary, and the principle of 'accommodation' – though it may be misapplied, as perhaps in the case of the Jesuit missionaries' adoption of Chinese customs – has always been practised by Christians since the earliest time.[23]

The theological office of the Church, then, may find itself in opposition to both the so-called political and pastoral offices. But equally, the political office may come into conflict with the other two offices. This office is, in fact, essential if the Church is to preserve its independence and freedom of action – as is illustrated by the Orthodox Church, 'which has lost its political life, while its doctrine, and its ritual and devotional system, have little that can be excepted against'.

Like 'a sovereign State', the Church has 'to consolidate her several portions, to enlarge her territory, to keep up and to increase her various populations in this ever-dying, ever-nascent world, in which to be stationary is to lose ground, and to repose is to fail'. So important is this aspect of the Church that a point of theology may at times actually be 'determined on its expediency relatively to the Church's Catholicity', that is, 'by the logic of facts, which at times overrides all positive laws and prerogatives, and reaches in its effective force to the very frontiers of immutable truths'.[24] While not exaggerating this aspect of the Church, as was usual in the theology of his day, Newman refuses to ignore or downplay the institutional aspect of the Church.

The Preface to the *Via Media* concludes with the reflection that 'whatever is great refuses to be reduced to human rule, and to be made consistent in its many aspects with itself'. There should be no cause for surprise, then, if the Church 'is an instance of the same law, presenting to us an admirable consistency and unity in word and deed, as her general characteristic, but crossed and discredited now and then by apparent anomalies'.[25] We might add that a Church, which is first and last a communion of vastly different persons, albeit baptized in the same Spirit, is hardly likely to exhibit that kind of orderliness and tidiness that is often vainly desiderated in place of the apparently unresolvable ambiguities and tensions that characterize Catholicism.

8

CHRISTIANITY AS THE
PRESENCE OF PERSONS

The severity of Newman's published sermons, which means principally his Anglican sermons which outnumber the relatively few Catholic sermons he composed for formal delivery and publication, has often been commented upon in critical terms. Thus Hilda Graef has accused him, as an Anglican, of overemphasizing the fear rather than the love of God, of lacking joy, of preaching 'a perpetual Lent', of an unchristian rigidity, of an unemotional detachment which is more Stoical than Christian. Graef acknowledges that the strictness of the Anglican preaching was shared by other Tractarians and was at least partly due to a reaction both against the worldly Christianity of an established religion and against the emotionalism of the Evangelical revival with its stress on feelings. She also admits that the severity was tempered by the great doctrine of the indwelling of the Holy Spirit, in teaching which, she says, Newman reached 'truly mystical heights'.[1] But here, I think, she is mistaken: it is not so much that this doctrine *tempers* as that it is the *cause* of the severity.

There were, of course, a number of factors involved, and certainly Newman's strong reaction against the Evangelicalism which had so powerfully influenced him in his adolescent conversion of 1816 is particularly important. Newman came to think that a theology which so stressed faith as against works is bound to have an antinomian tendency: if all that really counts is being justified by faith, then one's actual moral and spiritual state may seem practically irrelevant.

Moreover, a preoccupation with the faith-experience itself easily leads to a certain narcissistic introspectiveness. But when all has been said that needs to be said about Newman's criticism of Evangelical Christianity and the kind of moral earnestness and zeal that any religious revival like the Tractarian Movement inevitably gives rise to, there remains the doctrine of the indwelling of the Holy Spirit, which Newman had discovered for himself in the New Testament and the Greek Fathers, and which he saw as the foundation of the Christian life. Newman took with the utmost seriousness St Paul's teaching that the Christian is the temple of the Holy Spirit; and it is, I believe, this understanding that lies at the heart of his own uncompromising spirituality.

On the one hand the intimate presence of the Holy Spirit carries with it the most momentous possibilities for personal sanctification. For Christians, Newman preaches,

> have a spiritual principle in us, if we did but exert it, so great, so wondrous, that all the powers in the visible world, all the conceivable forces and appetites of matter, all the physical miracles which are at this day in process of discovery, almost superseding time and space, dispensing with numbers, and rivalling mind, all these powers of nature are nothing to this gift within us.[2]

However, it is not just that the failure to take advantage of such an extraordinary gift carries a special moral responsibility, but that this principle is not in the least abstract but consists in a person or rather persons, namely Christ, who comes to us through his Spirit, so that 'Christ is present in that heart which He visits with His grace'.[3] Sin, therefore, for a Christian is not merely the transgression of a law or moral principle but is in effect a personal insult, as being an offence against the person of Christ whose deeply intimate presence in the Christian is guaranteed through the indwelling of the Holy Spirit. Taking this cardinal New Testament doctrine as literally as Newman does leads him to regard sin as practically tantamount to sacrilege. Not merely the infringement of a norm or the lapse from a standard, sin takes on an alarmingly personal character. Nor is it simply an offence against an *absent* person, since, as we have already seen, Newman has a vivid awareness that since the resurrection and the descent of the Holy Spirit at Pentecost Christ is actually more really present than when he was here in his earthly presence. It is true that at the ascension the Son returned to the Father, but in his stead came 'the Eternal Love whereby the Father and the Son have dwelt in each other',[4] that is to say, the Holy Spirit, the third person of the Trinity. To think that Christ has left the world because he is no longer physically present is to ignore the fact that he is now present by and through his Spirit – more truly here indeed since now he is personally present to countless individuals. For a Christian, then, to sin is to defy or ignore the Christ who is closer and more intimately present than he was even to the Apostles in his earthly life. Consequently, for Newman, sin takes on the character of deeply personal rejection, with far more serious consequences than any impersonal law-breaking could ever have.

Newman himself powerfully makes the point in a passage in the Anglican *Lectures on the Doctrine of Justification* when he contrasts the 'more awakening and fearful doctrine' of the indwelling Spirit with other, more external views of justification, and points out the moral implications.

> For to what does it point as the great and immediate condition of justification? to faith and holiness of our own? or, on the other hand, to the mere title of righteousness, which cannot be literally approached or profaned by us? no, – but to the glorious Shekinah of the Word Incarnate, as to the true wedding garment in which the soul must be dressed. Does not such a view far increase, instead of diminishing, our responsibilities? does it not make us more watchful and more obedient, while it comforts and elevates? . . . When are we the more likely to keep awake and be sober, when we have a present treasure now to lose, or a distant reward to gain? Is it not more dreadful, when evil thoughts

assail us . . . to reflect (if the words may be used) that
we bear God within us, as the Martyr Ignatius expresses
it, that He is grieved by us . . . according as we carry or
renounce His Cross, – I say, has not this thought more
of persuasiveness in it to do and suffer for Him than
the views of doctrine which have spread among us? is it
not more constraining than that which considers that
the Gospel comes to us in name not in power; deeper,
and more sacred than a second, which makes its heavenly grace a matter of purchase and trade; more glow-
ing than a third, which depresses it almost to the chill
temperature of natural religion?[5]

Or, as he puts it elsewhere, it is because 'soul and body
become, by the indwelling of the Word, so elevated above
their natural state, so sacred, that to profane them is a
sacrilege'.[6]

Apart from his heightened sense of the divine indwelling
in the individual Christian, there is another reason for Newman's severe spirituality, and that is his deep consciousness
of the actual slavery of sin to which Christians are in fact
subjected in spite of enjoying free will. The incompatibility
of the two lies at the heart of Newman's preaching. Thus,
on the one hand, holiness ought to be the result of baptism,
as the New Testament implies with its 'one broad idea of a
state of salvation . . . not of sinning and being forgiven, but
of holiness'.[7] But, on the other hand, the facts are so often
so different. How does one reconcile the sacramental divinization of the Christian with his or her actual sinful life?
Newman's answer is that although we do indeed enjoy personal freedom, at least in principle, still, in practice, this
freedom is restricted by the ways in which we exercise it.
The problem is that while we are in theory free agents, in
practice we are so often the slaves of our own past actions.
The more we make the right choices in the present, the
freer we become to live the life of the Spirit. 'Is not holiness
the result of many patient, repeated efforts after obedience,
gradually working on us, and first modifying and then changing our hearts?'[8]

The freedom of the human person is an absolutely fundamental Christian tenet, so much so that the denial of hell is essentially the denial of the human right to reject God, a right which must be retained in principle if the doctrine of free will is to mean anything. It is partly because Newman is so anxious to uphold the dignity of the human person that he insists so sternly on the vital significance of the most apparently insignificant acts. For he sees only too clearly how we are conditioned and restricted by the habits and dispositions that our individual actions combine to create. So much hangs on small actions of seemingly little consequence. Thus one 'apparently small defect will influence your whole spirit and judgment in all things', since

> your judgment of persons, and of events, and of actions, and of doctrines, and your spirit towards God and man, your faith in the high truths of the Gospel, and your knowledge of your duty, all depend in a strange way on this strict endeavour to observe the whole law, on this self-denial in those little things in which obedience is a self-denial.[9]

An important reason why this is so is because human beings are notoriously slaves of habit. But our habits are formed by an accumulation of individual acts: 'there is the most close and remarkable connexion between small observances and the permanence of our chief habits and practices.'[10] Thus, Newman observes, 'men do not lose their souls by some one extraordinary act, but by a course of acts'.[11] For a person's character is formed by their habits, which, if they are sinful, 'clog [the will] in each particular exercise of it'.[12] Equally, on the other hand, since 'no habit is formed at once ... the flame of religion in the heart' needs to be 'purified and strengthened by long practice and experience'.[13] The unexciting truth is that it is only by '*systematically*' trying to be good that we become good.[14] But if it is difficult to build up good habits, once they are built up virtue becomes almost effortless. For, as 'habits of holiness are matured, principle, reason, and self-discipline are unnecessary; a moral instinct takes their place in the breast,

or rather, to speak more reverently, the Spirit is sovereign
there. There is no calculation, no struggle, no self-regard,
no investigation of motives. We act from love.'[15] It then
becomes possible to live quite easily and naturally in intimate
union with the indwelling Spirit:

> Then we do everything thankfully and joyfully, when we
> are temples of Christ, with His Image set up in us. Then
> it is that we mix with the world without loving it, for
> our affections are given to another. We can bear to look
> on the world's beauty, for we have no heart for it. We
> are not disturbed at its frowns, for we live not in its
> smiles. We rejoice in the House of Prayer, because He
> is there 'whom our soul loveth'. We can condescend to
> the poor and lowly, for they are the presence of Him
> who is Invisible. We are patient in bereavement,
> adversity, or pain, for they are Christ's tokens.[16]

Just as it is the indwelling of the Holy Spirit that makes
sin for a Christian practically a sacrilege, so by the same
token, of course, it is the indwelling Spirit who is the source
of holiness, for Christ 'brings us into it by coming to us
through His Spirit; and, as His Spirit is holy, we are holy, if
we are in the state of grace. Christ is present in that heart
which He visits with His grace.'[17] And the reason why so few
Christians achieve any real holiness is because 'out of the
whole number of persons blessed with the means of grace,
few only have duly availed them of this great benefit'.[18]

The Christian life, then, depends not only on Christ's
personal gift of himself in and through the presence of
the Holy Spirit, but also on the personal co-operation of the
individual Christian. Whatever the constraints and obstacles
created by human sinfulness, Newman stresses the role of
personal responsibility for the individual Christian gifted
with free will. This refusal simply to rest in the gift of the
Spirit is another very important reason for the sternness of
the Anglican sermons. Holiness, Newman insists, has to be
'wrought out of sin, the result of a continued struggle, –
not spontaneous nature, but habitual self-command'. It is
attained 'through infirmity, because man's very condition

is a fallen one, and in passing out of the county of sin, he necessarily passed through it'.[19] Even the smallest victories over sin are cause for rejoicing:

> if, for all our infirmities, we can point to some occasions on which we have sacrificed anything for God's service, or to any habit of sin or evil tendency of nature which we have more or less overcome, or to any habitual self-denial which we practise, or to any work which we have accomplished to God's honour and glory.[20]

We have God's presence within us, but 'what we want is the will; and it is our own fault that we have it not'. It is 'a very practical plain matter' that 'what we lack is the real, simple, earnest, sincere inclination and aim to use what God has given us, and what we have in us'. Have we ever actually '*willed*' to rid ourselves of a bad habit? To be sure, 'by nature we cannot will, but by grace we can': God gives us the power, that is, his Spirit, but we have to use the power he gives. And it is only by 'beginning by little and little' that we go on to '*will* great things'.[21] Indeed Christian conversion is necessarily a slow process:

> When men change their religious opinions really and truly, it is not merely their opinions that they change, but their hearts; and this evidently is not done in a moment – it is a slow work; nevertheless, though gradual, the change is often not uniform, but proceeds ... by fits and starts ... [22]

In any case, conversion is something that has to go on throughout the Christian life until the 'perfect Christian state' is reached, 'in which our duty and our pleasure are the same, when what is right and true is natural to us'.[23]

Yet another reason for Newman's severity is that he knows that the only remedy for ingrained sin is necessarily very painful. We are free to change, and yet we are not free. Once we have enslaved ourselves to a sinful habit, freedom from it can only be regained with the utmost difficulty. Thus 'a previous immoral life is ... a grievous permanent hindrance and a curse to a man, after he has turned to

God'.[24] Newman refuses to accept that the human person
does not possess freedom, but he is also convinced that the
ways in which we exercise this freedom impose very strong
constraints on the ways in which we may later choose to
exercise our free will. Each choice we make narrows the
scope of choice that we have in the future. It is precisely to
enlarge, to preserve the dignity of the person, that drastic
antidotes have to be applied. In particular, obviously, continual conversion involves painfully unending repentance:
because we sin constantly, we have to repent constantly, for
'sin neglected not only stains and infects the soul, but it
becomes habitual. It perverts and deforms the soul; it perma-
nently enfeebles, cripples, or mutilates us. Let us then rid
ourselves of it at once day by day, as of dust on our hands
and faces.' Newman's point is that our actions are habit-
forming, so that there is an urgent need to repent individual
sins, as otherwise they become self-repeating. We need to
repent not out of some neurotic guilt, but for the eminently
realistic reason that otherwise our freedom not to sin is
gradually and inexorably whittled away. It is psychological
insight not morbidity that leads Newman to urge:

> You cannot repent too much. Come to God day by day,
> intreating Him for all the sins of your whole life up to
> the very hour present. This is the way to keep your
> baptismal robe bright. Let it be washed as your garments
> of this world are, again and again; washed in the most
> holy, most precious, most awfully salutary of all streams,
> His blood, who is without blemish and without spot.[25]

Not even repentance, however, can remove the 'present
consequences' of 'past offences, whether outward or
inward', since 'sin *leaves* a burden upon the soul, which has
to be got rid of'.[26] Nor is repentance itself an easy matter:
'The truest kind of repentance as little comes at first, as
perfect conformity to any other part of God's Law. It is
gained by long practice – it will come at length.'[27] The fact
is that both conversion and repentance are so difficult as to
be impossible without God's grace: 'God alone can change
us; God alone can give us the desires, affections, principles,

views, and tastes which a change implies.' Humanly speaking, it is hard to imagine how such radical changes are possible as they go against all our natural inclinations:

> We do not like to be new-made; we are afraid of it; it is throwing us out of all our natural ways, of all that is familiar to us. We feel as if we should not *be* ourselves any longer, if we do not keep some portion of what we have been hitherto; and much as we prefer in general terms to wish to be changed, when it comes to the point, when particular instances of change are presented to us, we shrink from them, and are content to remain unchanged.

Psychologically, Newman warns his congregation, real repentance may be actually beyond their capacity: 'You cannot bear to be other than you are. Life would seem a blank to you, were you other.'[28]

An essential remedy for this incapacity is self-denial:

> Self-denial of some kind or other is involved . . . in the very notion of renewal and holy obedience. To change our hearts is to learn to love things which we do not naturally love – to unlearn the love of this world; but this involves, of course, a thwarting of our natural wishes and tastes. To be righteous and obedient implies self-command; but to possess power we must have gained it; nor can we gain it without a vigorous struggle, a persevering warfare against ourselves. The very notion of being religious implies self-denial, because by nature we do not love religion.[29]

To deny oneself is paradoxically to free oneself, since self-denial is the key to liberation from the constraints and pressures which restrict our freedom to choose what we know to be best:

> Nothing is so likely to corrupt our hearts, and to seduce us from God, as to surround ourselves with comforts, – to have things our own way, – to be the centre of a sort of world, whether of things animate or inanimate, which

minister to us. For then, in turn, we shall depend on them; they will become necessary to us; their very service and adulation will lead us to trust ourselves to them, and to idolize them.[30]

'Daily self-denials' help to strengthen one's 'general power of self-mastery', thus increasing one's personal freedom of action.[31] By the same token, the reason why obedience to God's commandments is so difficult is because the effort of past sins is to form 'sinful habits which hang upon [a person's] will, and clog it in each particular exercise of it'.[32] On the other hand, obedience creates good habits which in turn make obedience easier: 'if we strove to obey God's will in all things, we actually should be gradually training our hearts into the fulness of a Christian spirit'.[33] In other words, 'We must become what we are not; we must learn to love what we do not love, and practise ourselves in what is difficult.'[34] Like self-denial, obedience in little things is particularly important: 'such creatures are we, there is the most close and remarkable connexion between small observances and the permanence of our chief habits and practices'.[35] It is not surprising to find that Newman thinks that 'consistent obedience is a very rare endowment',[36] as our past sins are responsible for so much involuntary inconsistency: 'past years rise up against us in present offences; gross inconsistencies show themselves in our character'.[37] Often it is to 'single or forgotten sins' that 'are not improbably to be traced the strange inconsistencies of character which we often witness in our experience of life'.[38]

Newman emphasizes the importance of self-examination for moral freedom. For habitual sinfulness leads to self-deception: 'Conscience at first warns us against sin; but if we disregard it, it soon ceases to upbraid us; and thus sins, once known, in time become secret sins. It seems then . . . that the more guilty we are, the less we know it; for the oftener we sin, the less we are distressed at it.'[39] It is very dangerous, in particular, to imagine that it is only outward behaviour that really counts: 'Evil thoughts do us no harm, if recognized, if repelled, if protested against by the indignation and self-reproach of the mind. It is when we do not discuss them, when we admit them, when we cherish them, that they ripen into principles'.[40] The fact is that sin is self-propagating: 'When a man begins to do wrong, he cannot answer for himself how far he may be carried on... One false step forces him to another, for retreat is impossible.'[41] Unfortunately, once 'we have begun an evil course, we cannot retrace our steps'.[42] Indeed we might say that it is fortunate that we cannot realize the full implications of our sins: 'Did we see the complete consequences of any one sin, did we see how it spreads by the contagion of example and influence through the world, how many souls it injures, and what its eternal effects are, doubtless we should become speechless and motionless, as though we saw the flames of hell fire.'[43] Just as the sins of childhood imprint 'indelible hues' on one's character, so too

> when the mind is excited, thrown out of its ordinary state ... as if into that original unformed state when it was more free to choose good and evil, then in like manner it takes impressions, and those indelible ones, and withal most unconsciously, after the manner of childhood. This is one reason why a time of trial is often such a crisis in a man's spiritual history. It is a season when the iron is heated and malleable; one or two strokes serve to fashion it as a weapon for God or for Satan.

Past sins may also 'account for the strange way in which defects of character are buried in a man', until 'certain circumstances... bring them out'. Again, 'single sins indulged or neglected are often the cause of other defects of character, which seem to have no connexion with them, but which after all are rather symptomatic of the former, than themselves at the bottom of the mischief'. Everybody probably has 'some besetting sin or other, some infirmity, some temptation; and in resisting this lies their trial'.[44] We have involuntary sins 'which arise from our former habits of sin, though now long abandoned', but which nevertheless give 'a colour to our thoughts, words, and works', so that our 'former self clings' to us 'as a poisoned garment, and eats into' us.[45] There is only one way of avoiding the long-term effects of our sins:

> Never suffer sin to remain upon you; let it not grow old in you; wipe it off while it is fresh, else it will stain; let it not get ingrained; let it not eat its way in, and rust in you. It is of a consuming nature; it is like a canker; it will eat your flesh.[46]

So powerful are our habits that, positively, Newman even goes so far as to define grace in terms of habit: 'We do not know what we mean by a habit, except as a state or quality of mind *under* which we act in this or that particular way; it is a permanent power in the mind; and what is grace but this?' But whereas 'grace was to [Adam] instead of a habit', fallen man has to gain it 'by dent of exercise, working up towards it by religious acts'.[47] It is our responsibility, then, to make sure that we perform the right actions which will create the right habits: 'We have power over our deeds ... we have no direct power over our habits. Let us but secure our actions ... and our habits will follow.'[48] The possibility of spiritual progress is not after all so unreal: 'Who can say the heights to which in time men can proceed in all things, who beginning by little and little, yet in the distance shadow forth great things?'[49] But we must 'begin with the beginning' and not '*with* the end', for we have to 'mount up the heavenly ladder step by step'.[50] And so we shall make progress, even if imperceptibly: 'It is by going on quickly and steadily, with the thought of Him in our mind's eye, that by little and little we shall gain something of warmth, light, life, and love. We shall not perceive ourselves changing. It will be like the unfolding of leaves in spring.'[51]

When all has been said that needs to be said about Newman's psychological insight into the nature of a person's moral freedom, we should never suppose that the heart of his spirituality lies anywhere else than in the person of Jesus Christ. The fundamental driving-force behind the Christian life is the great call to self-abandonment – 'a surrender of ourselves, soul and body, to Him'.[52] And this, in turn,

of course, for Newman derives from the doctrine of the
divine indwelling, for we are not called to abandon ourselves
to an external reality but to a person already intimately
present to us, that is, if we are prepared to accept his presence. The true Christian

> admits Christ into the shrine of his heart; whereas
> others wish in some way or other, to be by themselves,
> to have a home, a chamber, a tribunal, a throne, a self
> where God is not, – a home within them which is not
> a temple, a chamber which is not a confessional, a
> tribunal without a judge, a throne without a king; – that
> self may be king and judge; and that the Creator may
> rather be dealt with and approached as though a second
> party, instead of His being that true and better self,
> of which self itself should be but an instrument and
> minister.[53]

This is the essence of the Christian vocation to a personal
relationship with Christ: 'The one thing, which is all in all
to us, is to live in Christ's presence; to hear His voice, to see
His countenance.'[54]

A personal relationship demands personal communication, and for a Christian it is prayer which is *divine* con-
verse'.[55] But because of the indwelling of the Holy Spirit,
our prayer is really that of the Holy Spirit. Indeed, it is
prayer which above all reveals to us that the Spirit is in fact
present in us: for, 'as our bodily life discovers itself by its
activity, so is the presence of the Holy Spirit in us discovered
by a spiritual activity; and this activity is the spirit of continual
prayer. Prayer is to spiritual life what the beating of the pulse
and the drawing of the breath are to the life of the body.'[56]
The reason contemplative prayer does not come naturally
to us is that the fall has deprived us of 'man's happiness in
Paradise, not to think about himself or to be conscious of
himself' – 'for what is contemplation but a resting in the
thought of God to the forgetfulness of self?'[57] Meditation on
the person of Christ is essential, and Newman urges the
importance of

thinking habitually and constantly of Him and of His deeds and sufferings . . . And by this, and nothing short of this, will our hearts come to feel as they ought. We have stony hearts, hearts as hard as the highways; the history of Christ makes no impression on them. And yet, if we would be saved, we must have tender, sensitive, living hearts; our hearts must be broken, must be broken up like ground, and dug, and watered, and tended, and cultivated, till they become as gardens, gardens of Eden, acceptable to our God, gardens in which the Lord God may walk and dwell; filled, not with briars and thorns, but with all sweet-smelling and useful plants, with heavenly trees and flowers. The dry and barren waste must burst forth into springs of living water . . . we must have what we have not by nature, faith and love; and how is this to be effected . . . but by godly and practical meditation through the day?[58]

The prayer Newman has in mind is not general reflection on abstract doctrine but something of a much more personally contemplative kind, that is, 'holding communion with God, or living in God's sight', which 'may be done all through the day, wherever we are, and is commanded us as the duty, or rather the characteristic, of those who are really servants and friends of Jesus Christ'.[59]

Since Christianity is what Newman calls a 'social religion' and involves Christians praying together in the communion of baptized persons that is the Church, 'united prayer is necessarily of an intercessory character, as being offered for each other and for the whole, and for self as one of the whole'. But there is also a profoundly theological reason why the Christian must practise intercessory prayer: 'He is made after the pattern and in the fulness of Christ – he is what Christ is. Christ intercedes above, and he intercedes below.'[60]

Although a personal relationship with Christ lies at the heart of the Christian life, it would be quite unchristian only 'to rest in the thought of two and two only absolute and luminously self-evident beings, myself and my Creator', as 'childish imaginations', reinforced later by the Calvinistic doctrine of 'final perseverance', induced the youthful Newman to do.[61] The individual Christian's relation to God is inseparable from the communion of other Christians. Not only that, but it is a characteristically Newmanian theme that our charity towards others is formed and influenced by our own particular personal friendships. As Newman likes to point out, Christ himself had 'a private friend', the beloved disciple St John:

> and this shows us ... that there is nothing contrary to the spirit of the Gospel, nothing inconsistent with the fulness of Christian love, in having our affections directed in an especial way towards certain objects, towards those whom the circumstances of our past life, or some peculiarities of character, have endeared to us.

Newman has no time for those 'who have supposed Christian love was so diffusive as not to admit of concentration upon individuals; so that we ought to love all men equally ... that the love of many is something superior to the love of one or two'. On the contrary, he recommends that 'the best preparation for loving the world at large, and loving it duly and wisely, is to cultivate an intimate friendship and affection towards those who are immediately about us ... to love our brethren according to the flesh, [is] the first step towards considering all men our brethren'. And so Newman even insists that 'the love of our private friends is the only preparatory exercise for the love of all men'. To 'talk magnificently about loving the whole human race with a comprehensive affection, of being the friends of all mankind, and the like', Newman dismisses contemptuously as 'nothing more than unstable feelings, the mere offspring of an indulged imagination', for 'This is not to love men, it is but to talk about love. – The real love of man *must* depend on practice, and therefore, must begin by exercising itself on our friends around us, otherwise it will have no existence.'[62]

If Christian charity depends ultimately upon our ability to love actual individual persons, love of God, on the other hand, at least as it is expressed in one important traditional form, demands a particular detachment from any other human person. In the constant discussion today about the practicality and value of the celibacy law of the Latin rite in the Roman Catholic Church, it is worth noting that it is always the more negative word *celibacy*, or unmarried state, rather than the more positive word *virginity*, meaning a state of consecrated chastity, that is used. And the emphasis always seems to be on the fact that freedom from marriage and family enables the priest to be more available for the service of the people. Critics of the present system naturally point out that the celibacy requirement clearly deprives the Church of many excellent candidates for the ministerial priesthood, whose contribution would more than make up for any loss of availability, particularly as the really pressing need is for more priests for the celebration of the Eucharist. The lack of close personal ties that gives the priest a greater freedom for apostolic and pastoral work was certainly something that greatly impressed Newman long before the Tractarian Movement began. Already in 1816, the year of his first important conversion, a 'deep imagination... took possession' of him that it would be God's will that he should 'lead a single life', an 'anticipation' that was 'more or less connected' with the idea that his 'calling in life would require such a sacrifice as celibacy involved; as, for instance, missionary work among the heathen'.[63] As he became increasingly high church and perturbed at the dangers posed to the Church of England, he came to feel 'more strongly than ever the necessity of there being men in the Church, like the Roman Catholic friars, free from all obstacles to their devoting themselves to its defence'.[64] He was anxious at least that 'there should be among the clergy enough unmarried, to give a character of strength to the whole – and that therefore, every one should ask himself whether he is called to [be] celibate'. At a time of crisis the Church needed soldiers ready for action – not, he commented sarcastically, 'a whole camp of women at its heels, foreby brats'! What was needed was a group of totally dedicated clergy, especially since 'the only way' of 'evangelizing' the new industrial towns was through what he called 'monastic orders':

> great towns will never be evangelized merely by the
> parochial system. They are beyond the sphere of the
> parish priest, burdened as he is with the endearments
> and anxieties of a family, and the secular restraints and
> engagements of the Establishment. The unstable multitude cannot be influenced and ruled except by uncommon means, by the evident sight of disinterested and
> self-denying love, and elevated firmness. The show of
> domestic comfort, the decencies of furniture and
> apparel, the bright hearth and the comfortable table,
> (good and innocent as they are in their place,) are as
> ill-suited to the missionary of a town population as to
> an Apostle.

However, Newman still thought that 'country parsons ought, as a general rule, to be married'. And he was aware too that clergy wives were 'useful in a parish, and that in a way in which no *man* can rival them'. He was also conscious that celibacy was 'a high state of life, to which the multitude of men cannot aspire', even though he could not claim that 'they who adopt it are necessarily better than others'. But he still believed it was the 'noblest' way of life.[65] What did he mean by that?

He surely meant more than even the self-sacrifice involved in giving one's life to the mission of the Church. He had, in fact, been much influenced by his friend Hurrell Froude's 'high severe idea of the intrinsic excellence of Virginity'.[66] This was the vocation to which he increasingly felt himself called as an Anglican, that is, to virginity rather than just celibacy, if one may make the distinction: 'God ... has so framed my mind that I am in a great measure beyond the sympathies of other people, and thrown upon Himself ...'[67] As a Roman Catholic, Newman did not question the discipline of the Latin rite which requires its priests to be celibate; the same reasons, as we have seen, had already impressed him as an Anglican, that is to say, celibacy seemed to be the most suitable state for a priest, although it was not of course of the essence of the priesthood.[68] But he also understood as an Anglican that the pragmatic convenience of celibacy which frees a person from the ties of marriage and family for a further commitment to the service of the Church is not quite the same as the ideal of virginity, whereby the lack of intimate human affection is a means for the human heart to find effective fulfilment in the exclusive love of God. As a poem he wrote in 1833 puts it, 'Thrice bless'd are they, who feel their loneliness', for 'sick at heart, beyond the veil they fly, / Seeking His Presence, who alone can bless.'[69] Two decades later, after he had seen how institutional celibacy in the Roman Catholic Church is all too often lived out in practice, he was to declare, 'To make a single life its own end, to adopt it simply and solely for its own sake, I do not know whether such a state of life is more melancholy or more unamiable, melancholy from its unrequited desolateness and unamiable from the pride and self-esteem on which it is based.' But:

> This is not the Virginity of the Gospel – it is not a state of independence or isolation, or dreary pride, or barren indolence, or crushed affections; man is made for sympathy, for the interchange of love! for self-denial for the sake of another dearer to him than himself. The Virginity of the Christian soul is a marriage with Christ.[70]

Celibacy, then, for Newman is not simply a means towards greater apostolic effectiveness, if only because without the right affectivity such a state will prove to be destructive and self-destructive. Nor is it merely an impersonal sign of the Kingdom of God. Rather, for Newman celibacy is bound up with that particular exclusive relationship with Christ which alone satisfies the deepest needs of the human heart.

9

DEATH AND THE 'GLANCE OF GOD'

Newman's spirituality of death centres on the idea of a personal encounter with God after this life, an encounter that he likes to describe in visual terms to emphasize how individual and personal it will be. For him the drama of death is fundamentally that then we shall, for better or for worse, see God 'as he really is', in St John's words.[1] This will be the joyful moment of fulfilment for those who truly love God, but for ordinary sinners it will be a more or less painful and shocking sight, since most people 'begin to lose sight of God' in this life through their failure to love or to want God:

> Like men who fall asleep, the real prospect still flits before them in their dreams, but out of shape and proportion, discoloured, crowded with all manner of fancies and untruths; and so they proceed in that dream of sin, more or less profound ... Death alone gives lively perceptions to the generality of men, who then see the very truth, such as they saw it before they began to sin, but more clear and more fearful.[2]

When we die we come before God, and the prospect of that encounter fills us with fear, not least because of the profoundly personal character of that meeting when we are met not so much with judgment as a judge:

> We are not merely to be rewarded or punished, we are to be judged. Recompense is to come upon our actions,

not by a mere general provision or course of nature, as it does at present, but from the Lawgiver himself in person. We have to stand before His righteous Presence, and that one by one. One by one we shall have to endure His holy and searching eye. At present we are in a world of shadows. What we see is not substantial. Suddenly it will be rent in twain and vanish away, and our Maker will appear. And then, I say, that first appearance will be nothing less than a personal intercourse between the Creator and every creature. He will look on us, while we look on Him.[3]

Thus the awful nature of our judgment at death lies in that supremely personal encounter with God, when, to use Newman's own fearfully simple words, 'He will look on us, while we look on Him'. In other words, the judgment consists in the look of divine love which reveals both who God is and what kind of a person we are.

One answer that Newman gives to the problem of hell is to suggest that to the unrepentant sinner heaven would in fact be a hell. Such a person would not only 'sustain a great disappointment' but would experience excruciating unhappiness: 'he could not *bear* the face of the living God; the Holy God would be no object of joy to him ... None but the holy one can look upon the Holy One; without holiness no man can endure to see the Lord.' And so far from representing eternal bliss, 'Heaven would be hell to an irreligious man', for 'if we wished to imagine a punishment for an unholy, reprobate soul, we perhaps could not fancy a greater than to *summon it to heaven*'.[4] It is characteristic of Newman to stress that such an existence would be one of total isolation and loneliness, cut off from all communication with other persons:

We know how unhappy we are apt to feel at present, when alone in the midst of strangers, or of men of different tastes and habits from ourselves. How miserable, for example, would it be to have to live in a foreign land, among a people whose faces we never saw before, and whose language we could not learn. And this is but a faint illustration of the loneliness of a man of earthly dispositions and tastes, thrust into the society of saints and angels. How forlorn would he wander through the courts of heaven! He would find no one like himself; he would see in every direction the marks of God's holiness, and these would make him shudder.

There is nothing abstract about this holiness, which again Newman conveys through that most personal expression of a person, the *look*:

> He would feel himself always in His presence. He could no longer turn his thoughts another way, as he does now, when conscience reproaches him. He would know that the Eternal Eye was ever upon him; and that Eye of holiness, which is joy and life to holy creatures, would seem to him an Eye of wrath and punishment.[5]

At death not only will we have to meet God's look, but we shall also see ourselves as we never did in our earthly lives. This sight will be our purgatory, as Newman seems to recognize in one of his Anglican sermons:

> Doubtless we must all endure that fierce and terrifying vision of our real selves, that last fiery trial of the soul before its acceptance, a spiritual agony and second death to all who are not then supported by the strength of Him who died to bring them safe through it, and in whom on earth they have believed.[6]

If it is only ourself that we can see because we are completely absorbed in ourself, then we are in effect in hell as Callista came to be persuaded – 'You will be yourself, shut up in yourself.'[7]

Writing as a Catholic about purgatory in *The Dream of Gerontius* (1865), Newman again envisages both the punishment and the purification in terms of the Creator's look of love, which will be a veritable torment to the soul as it regards the ingratitude of its own lovelessness:

> It is the face of the Incarnate God
> Shall smite thee with that keen and subtle pain;
> And yet the memory which it leaves will be
> A sovereign febrifuge to heal the wound;
> And yet without it will the wound provoke,
> And aggravate and widen it the more.

Purgatory is seen not as a penalty externally inflicted by God, but rather both the pain and the punishment are the vision of the loving God contrasted with the sight of one's own sinfulness:

> There is a pleading in His pensive eyes
> Will pierce thee to the quick, and trouble thee.
> And thou will hate and loathe thyself; for, though
> Now sinless, thou will feel that thou hast sinn'd,
> As never thou didst feel; and wilt desire
> To slink away, and hide thee from His sight:
> And yet will have a longing aye to dwell
> Within the beauty of His countenance.
> And these two pains, so counter and so keen, –
> The longing for Him, when thou seest Him not;
> The shame of self at thought of seeing Him! –
> Will be the veriest, sharpest purgatory.

The paradoxical nature of a torment that is bliss is summed up in the succinct couplet:

> O happy, suffering soul! for it is safe,
> Consumed, yet quicken'd by the glance of God.

And it is this deeply personal encounter with its Creator that the repentant soul welcomes as the price of and remedy for sin:

> Take me away, and in the lowest deep
> There let me be . . . [8]

One of the most famous passages in Newman's writings,

from *Parochial and Plain Sermons,* is about heaven rather than purgatory:

> After the fever of Life; after wearinesses and sicknesses; fightings and despondings; languor and fretfulness; struggling and failing, struggling and succeeding; after all the changes and chances of this troubled unhealthy state, at length comes death, at length the White Throne of God, at length the Beatific Vision.

The beatific vision is the sight of a personal God who is also a God of persons:

> After restlessness comes rest, peace, joy; – our eternal portion, if we be worthy; – the sight of the Blessed Three, the Holy One; the Three that bear witness in heaven . . . The Father God, the Son God, and the Holy Ghost God; the Father Lord, the Son Lord, and the Holy Ghost Lord; the Father uncreate, the Son uncreate, and the Holy Ghost uncreate; the Father incomprehensible, the Son incomprehensible, and the Holy Ghost incomprehensible. For there is one Person of the Father, another of the Son, and another of the Holy Ghost; and such as the Father is, such is the Son, and such is the Holy Ghost; and yet there are not three Gods, nor three Lords, nor three incomprehensibles, nor three uncreated; but one God, one Lord, one uncreated, and one incomprehensible.[9]

This magnificent vision of God, one in three persons, is the consummation and fulfilment of human life. It is a fitting note on which to end this study of the personalism of Newman's spirituality.

CONCLUSION

In the course of Newman's defence in the *Apologia* of his conversion to Catholicism, there occurs the following striking sentence, which in effect sums up the theme of this book: 'I am a Catholic by virtue of my believing in a God; and if I am asked why I believe in a God, I answer that it is because I believe in myself . . .'[1]

Starting from the position that religious faith involves the personal exercise of our own judgment and obedience to our individual conscience, Newman justifies belief in a personal God on the ground that it is only in such a God that the human person can find the meaning and fulfilment of their own existence and nature. This idea of a personal God arising out of self-reflection achieves historical realization in Jesus Christ, whose person is the subject of Christian revelation. The Son of God reveals the other two persons of the Trinity, and it is the Spirit of God as the mutual love of the Father and Son who makes Christ personally present in the Christian. This divine indwelling comes to us through the sacrament of baptism and is sustained especially by Christ's real presence in the Eucharist. It is because the Church, through which and into which we are baptized, is the communion of all those persons who have received the Holy Spirit through baptism, that the Church exhibits those problems and conflicts that inevitably arise out of the interaction of very diverse people with individual charisms and gifts, all of which are liable to different corruptions. The Christian life itself makes the highest demands on the believer, because it is centred not only on a personal God manifested in the person of Christ but on a profoundly personal relationship through Christ's indwelling in the Holy Spirit. And the judgment we receive at the end of our life is not an impersonal verdict but consists of a supreme personal encounter with Christ, whose 'look' or 'glance' of love is both our punishment and our reward.

We can see now why Newman can rest his belief in Catholicism on a belief in a personal God, which in turn he bases on his belief in his own existence and identity. If we take the human person seriously we are led on to believe in a personal God who manifests himself uniquely in the incarnate person of Christ, whose personal presence in individual Christians unites them in the body of his Church. Moreover it is this intimately personal reality which heightens the drama of both Christian life and death. Given that Christianity is essentially and fundamentally a religion of persons, for Newman its fullness is to be found in the sacramentality and communion of Catholicism, in which this personalism finds its most complete and concrete realization. And when at the end of his life Newman received the cardinal's hat, he confirmed his earliest insights into the deeply personal nature of the Christian religion by taking as his cardinalatial motto a saying from another great Christian humanist, St Francis de Sales, 'cor ad cor loquitur', 'heart speaks to heart'.

ABBREVIATIONS

Newman collected his works in a uniform edition of 36 volumes (1868–81). Until his death in 1890 he continued making minor textual changes in reprints of individual volumes in this edition, of which all the volumes from 1886 were published by Longmans, Green of London. References are usually to volumes in the uniform edition published after 1890 by Longmans, Green, which are distinguished from other editions by not including publication details in parentheses after the title.

Apo.	*Apologia pro Vita Sua,* ed. Martin J. Svaglic (Oxford: Clarendon Press, 1967)
Ari.	*The Arians of the Fourth Century*
Ath. i, ii	*Select Treatises of St Athanasius,* 2 vols
Call.	*Callista: A Tale of the Third Century*
DA	*Discussions and Arguments on Various Subjects*
Dev.	*An Essay on the Development of Christian Doctrine*
Diff. i, ii	*Certain Difficulties felt by Anglicans in Catholic Teaching,* 2 vols
Ess. i, ii	*Essays Critical and Historical,* 2 vols
GA	*An Essay in Aid of a Grammar of Assent,* ed. I. T. Ker (Oxford: Clarendon Press, 1985)
Jfc.	*Lectures on the Doctrine of Justification*
LD i-vi, xi-xxxi	*The Letters and Diaries of John Henry Newman,* ed. Charles Stephen Dessain *et al.,* vols i-vi (Oxford: Clarendon Press, 1978–84), xi-xxii (London: Nelson, 1961–72), xxiii-xxxi (Oxford: Clarendon Press, 1973–7)
LG	*Loss and Gain: The Story of a Convert*
MD	*Meditations and Devotions of the Late Cardinal Newman*

	(London: Longmans, Green, 1893)
Mix.	*Discourses addressed to Mixed Congregations*
NO	*Newman the Oratorian: His Unpublished Oratory Papers*, ed. Placid Murray, OSB (Dublin: Gill and Macmillan, 1969)
OS	*Sermons preached on Various Occasions*
PS i-viii	*Parochial and Plain Sermons*, 8 vols
Phil.N. i, ii	*The Philosophical Notebook of John Henry Newman*, ed. Edward Sillem, 2 vols (Louvain: Nauwelaerts, 1969–70)
Prepos.	*Present Position of Catholics in England*
SD	*Sermons bearing on Subjects of the Day*
SN	*Sermon Notes of John Henry Cardinal Newman, 1849–1878*, ed. Fathers of the Birmingham Oratory (London: Longmans, Green, 1913)
TT	*Tracts Theological and Ecclesiastical*
US	*Fifteen Sermons preached before the University of Oxford*
VM i, ii	*The Via Media*, 2 vols
VV	*Verses on Various Occasions*

NOTES

1 The Personal Nature of Religious Belief

1 *LD* i. 219, 226.
2 *Prepos.* 283–4.
3 *US* 188, 190–3, 197–200.
4 *US* 225–7, 230, 234, 236, 239, 250.
5 *Apo.* 31.
6 *Dev.* 107, 123, 327.
7 *LD* xi. 289.
8 *LD* xv. 457–8.
9 *GA* 187, 189–90.
10 *GA* 195–6, 202.
11 *LD* xxiv. 275–6.
12 *GA* 205–8.
13 *GA* 221, 223, 226, 232–33, 245.
14 *GA* 264, 266.

2 A Personal God

1 Aidan Nichols, OP, *A Grammar of Consent: The Existence of God in Christian Tradition* (Edinburgh: T. and T. Clark, 1991), 1, 19, 35.
2 Romans 2:15.
3 *GA* 251, 72–6.
4 Martin C. D'Arcy, *No Absent God: The Relations between God and Self* (London: Routledge and Kegan Paul, 1962), 37.
5 *Phil.N.* ii. 59.
6 *PS* ii. 18.
7 *Call.* 314–15.
8 *OS* 65.

9   *Apo.* 216–17.
10 *Call.* 293.
11 *Call.* 131–2.
12 *Call.* 219–21.
13 *Call.* 326.
14 *Call.* 265.
15 *Call.* 292.
16 Nichols, op. cit., p. 37.
17 *GA* 253, 256.
18 *Apo.* 216–17.
19 *PS* v. 314–16.
20 *Confessions,* I.1.
21 *PS* v. 316–19, 324–5.
22 *PS* v. 325–6.
23 *PS* vi. 339–40.
24 *PS* iii. 124.
25 *Apo.* 18.
26 *PS* i. 19–20.
27 *PS* v. 315, 321.

3   The Person of Jesus Christ

1   *GA* 277.
2   *GA* 298–9.
3   *GA* 313.
4   *LD* xxvi. 87.
5   *SN* 125.
6   *PS* ii. 171.
7   *PS* ii. 161–2.
8   *PS* ii. 167, 169.
9   *LD* ii. 308.
10 *LD* v. 327.
11 *PS* iii. 130–1.
12 For a careful response to the criticism, *see* Roderick Strange,
    'Newman and the Mystery of Christ' in Ian Ker and Alan G.
    Hill, eds, *Newman After a Hundred Years* (Oxford: Clarendon
    Press, 1990), 323–36.
13 *MD* 360.
14 *MD* 412.
15 *Dev.* 35–6, 324.

16 *See* Ian Ker, *Newman and the Fullness of Christianity* (Edinburgh: T. and T. Clark, 1993), ch. 5.
17 *PS* i. 176.
18 *PS* ii. 32.
19 *Mix.* 321–2, 358.
20 *Call.* 221, 326.
21 James Anthony Froude, *Short Studies on Great Subjects*, fourth series (New York: Charles Scribner's Sons, 1910), 188.
22 *PS* vi. 73.
23 *Mix.* 325–9.
24 *Mix.* 329, 331, 334–5, 341.
25 See Michael Moore, 'Newman and the Motif of Intellectual Pain in Hopkins' "Terrible Sonnets" ', *Mosaic*, 12/4 (1979), 40; cf. Norman H. Mackenzie, ed., *The Poetical Works of Gerard Manley Hopkins* (Oxford: Clarendon Press, 1990), 451.
26 *PS* i. 177–8, 186.
27 *PS* i. 185, 187.
28 *PS* i. 298.
29 *PS* ii. 279–80, 286.
30 *PS* i. 303–4.
31 *PS* i. 322–3.
32 *PS* ii. 70–1.
33 *PS* vi. 45.
34 *PS* iv. 241–2, 245–9.
35 *OS* 40.
36 *OS* 42–3.
37 *SD* 312–13; cf. *OS* 51–3.
38 *SD* 312–13.
39 *OS* 52–3.

4   The Christian Revelation – Personal or Propositional?

1 *DA* 388.
2 *US* 330.
3 *DA* 130–1, 134.
4 *DA* 296.
5 *Diff.* ii. 236.
6 *Ari.* 36–7.
7 *Apo.* 36–7.
8 *Ari.* 145–6.
9 *Ess.* i. 41–2.

10   *Jfc.* 316.
11   *US* 331–2, 336.
12   *GA* 82–3.
13   *LD* xxiii. 99–100.
14   *LD* xxiii. 105.
15   *LD* xxv. 418.
16   *Diff.* ii. 236, 222.

5   The Persons of the Trinity

1   *TT* 167–8, 170–1, 178–9.
2   *PS* vi. 58.
3   *PS* i. 176.
4   *PS* ii. 142–3.
5   *PS* ii. 221.
6   *PS* ii. 222.
7   *PS* iv. 248–9.
8   *PS* v. 138–9.
9   *PS* v. 139.
10   *SD* 141.
11   *PS* vi. 124, 126.
12   *PS* v. 139–40.
13   *PS* ii. 222, 35.
14   *Jfc.* 34.
15   *PS* iv. 168.
16   *PS* v. 156–8.
17   *PS* vi. 184.
18   *Jfc.* 136–8, 154.
19   *VV* 364.

6   Christ's Personal Presence in the Sacraments

1   *John Henry Newman* (London: A. and C. Black, 1966), 20.
2   cf. *Dev.* 325: 'The doctrine of the Incarnation is the announce-
ment of a divine gift conveyed in a material and visible
medium, it being thus that heaven and earth are in the Incarnation united. That is, it establishes in the very idea of Christianity the *sacramental* principle as its characteristic.'
3   *Ath.* ii. 193.

4   *PS* iii. 271.
5   *PS* iii. 283.
6   *PS* viii. 57.
7   *Jfc.* 323.
8   *See* especially the classic work by Henri de Lubac, *Catholicism: Christ and the Common Destiny of Man* (Eng. tr. 1950).
9   *PS* vii. 235.
10 *PS* v. 10–11.
11 *PS* vii. 159.
12 *PS* vi. 151.
13 *PS* v. 283.
14 *PS* i. 275.
15 *PS* iv. 148.
16 *PS* vi. 136–7.
17 *LD* v. 47.
18 *DA* 388.
19 *LD* xi. 131.
20 *LD* xi. 129, 65.
21 *LD* xi. 249–50, 252–4.
22 *LG* 427.
23 *LD* xii. 224.

7   The Church a Communion of Persons

1   *PS* iii. 224; v. 41.
2   *PS* iii. 270.
3   *PS* iv. 170, 174, 171.
4   *PS* vii. 232–3.
5   *PS* iv. 169.
6   *VM* ii. 422.
7   *PS* iii. 220.
8   *PS* vii. 36–8.
9   *Diff.* ii. 89.
10 *Ess.* ii. 53–4.
11 *LD* xx. 465.
12 *LD* xxvii. 139.
13 *LD* xxv. 203–4.
14 *LD* xxvii. 265.
15 *VM* i. pp. xl–xliii, xlvii–xlviii.
16 *VM* i. pp. lxvi–lxxi, lxxiv.
17 *Apo.* 224–6.

18 *Apo.* 226, 229–31.

19 *Apo.* 231–3.

20 *Apo.* 237–41.

21 *VM* i. pp. xxxviii, xli, xlviii-l, lii-lvi.

22 *LD* xxv. 31–2; xxii. 99.

23 *VM* i. pp. lxxv-lxxxvi.

24 *VM* i. pp. lxxx-lxxxi, lxxxviii.

25 *VM* i. p. xciv.

8 Christianity as the Presence of Persons

1 Hilda Graef, *God and Myself: The Spirituality of John Henry Newman* (London: P. Davies, 1967), 53, 54, 59, 65–6, 68, 69, 75–6.

2 *PS* v. 345.

3 *PS* v. 181.

4 *PS* ii.229.

5 *Jfc.* 190–1

6 *Ath.* ii. 195

7 *PS* iv. 107–8.

8 *PS* i. 11.

9 *PS* i. 69.

10 *PS* i. 252.

11 *PS* iii. 217.

12 *PS* i. 167.

13 *PS* i. 142.

14 *PS* i. 145.

15 *PS* v. 109.

16 *PS* v. 340.

17 *PS* v. 179, 181.

18 *PS* v. 254.

19 *PS* v. 210.

20 *PS* v. 220.

21 *PS* v. 343, 348, 349, 354.

22 *PS* viii. 225.

23 *PS* iv. 4.

24 *PS* ii. 100.

25 *PS* v. 207–8.

26 *PS* iv. 96.

27 *PS* iii. 98.

28 *PS* v. 241, 350.

29 *PS* vii. 86.
30 *PS* vii. 98.
31 *PS* i. 69.
32 *PS* i. 167.
33 *PS* i. 233.
34 *PS* iv. 15.
35 *PS* i. 252.
36 *PS* ii. 272–3.
37 *PS* i. 10.
38 *PS* iv. 42.
39 *PS* i. 51.
40 *PS* iv. 72.
41 *PS* iii. 67.
42 *PS* iv. 35.
43 *PS* iii. 295.
44 *PS* iv. 41–5.
45 *PS* v. 212–13.
46 *PS* v. 206.
47 *PS* v. 108.
48 *PS* ii. 161.
49 *PS* vi. 354.
50 *PS* vi. 34.
51 *PS* vi. 43.
52 *PS* i. 324.
53 *PS* v. 226.
54 *PS* vi. 30.
55 *PS* iv. 227–8
56 *PS* vii. 209.
57 *PS* viii. 259.
58 *PS* vi. 41–2.
59 *PS* vii. 204.
60 *PS* iii. 352–3, 363.
61 *Apo.* 18.
62 *PS* ii. 52–5.
63 *Apo.* 20.
64 *LD* ii. 133.
65 *LD* iii. 23, 43, 70, 107; v. 17, 346; *DA* 42.
66 *Apo.* 34.
67 *LD* v. 313.
68 *See LD* iv. 371; xix. 540.
69 *VV* 104.
70 *NO* 277.

9   Death and the 'Glance of God'

1   1 John 3:2.
2   *PS* vii. 127.
3   *PS* v. 3–4.
4   *PS* i. 5–7.
5   *PS* i. 7–8.
6   *PS* i. 48–9.
7   *Call.* 219.
8   *VV* 358–60, 366.
9   *PS* vi. 369–70

Conclusion

1   *Apo.* 180.

SELECT BIBLIOGRAPHY

1 Primary Sources

Apart from the works referred to in this book and cited in the list of Abbreviations (p. 112), the following posthumously published volumes should also be noted.

John Henry Newman: Autobiographical Writings, ed. Henry Tristram (London and New York: Sheed and Ward, 1956).
Catholic Sermons of Cardinal Newman, ed. at Birmingham Oratory (London: Burns and Oates, 1957); also published as *Faith and Prejudice and Other Unpublished Sermons of Cardinal Newman* (New York: Sheed and Ward, 1956).
John Henry Newman: Sermons 1824–1843, vol. i, ed. Placid Murray, OSB (Oxford: Clarendon Press, 1991).

2 Secondary Sources

Biemer, Günter and Fries, Heinrich, eds — *Internationale Cardinal-Newman-Studien*, vol. xii: 'Christliche Heiligkeit als Lehre und Praxis nach John Henry Newman/Newman's Teaching on Christian Holiness' (Sigmaringendorf: regio Verlag Glock and Lutz, 1988).

Blehl, Vincent Ferrer, S. J. — 'Divine Call and Human Response: John Henry Newman on Prayer', *The Way*, October 1982, pp. 297–306.

Bouyer, Louis	*Newman: His Life and Spirituality* (London: Burns and Oates, 1958).
–	*Newman's Vision of Faith* (San Francisco: Ignatius Press, 1986).
Boyce, Philip	*Spiritual Exodus of John Henry Newman and Thérèse of Lisieux* (Dublin and Manchester: Carmelite Centre of Spirituality/Koinonia, 1979).
Davies, Horton	*Worship and Theology in England: From Newman to Martineau, 1850–1900* (Princeton: Princeton University Press, 1962).
Dessain, Charles Stephen	*John Henry Newman* (London: A. and C. Black, 1966)
–	*The Spirituality of John Henry Newman* (Minneapolis: Winston Press, 1977); also published as *Newman's Spiritual Themes* (Dublin: Veritas Publications, 1977).
–	'Newman's Spirituality: Its Value Today' in Charles Davis, ed., *English Spiritual Writers* (London: 1961), reprinted from *The Clergy Review,* 45 (May 1960), 257–82.
Graef, Hilda	*God and Myself: The Spirituality of John Henry Newman* (London: P. Davies, 1967).
Griffiths, Eric	'Newman: The Foolishness of Preaching' in Ian Ker and Alan G. Hill, eds, *Newman After a Hundred Years* (Oxford: Clarendon Press, 1990), 63–91.

Ker, Ian

John Henry Newman: A Biography (Oxford: Clarendon Press, 1988).

–

The Achievement of John Henry Newman (Notre Dame: University of Notre Dame Press, 1990; London: Collins, 1990).

–

Newman on Being a Christian (Notre Dame: University of Notre Dame Press, 1990; London: HarperCollins, 1991).

Lamm, William R

The Spiritual Legacy of Newman (Milwaukee: Bruce Publishing Co., 1934).

Reidy, James

'Newman and Christian Humanism,' *Renascence*, 44 (Summer 1992), 249–64.

Rowell, Geoffrey

'The Roots of Newman's Scriptural Holiness: Some Formative Influences on Newman's Spirituality' in Heinrich Fries and Werner Becker, eds, *Newman Studien*, 10 (Heroldsberg, Nürnberg: Glock and Lutz, 1978), 13–20.

Tristram, Henry

'With Newman at Prayer' in *John Henry Newman: Centenary Essays* (London: Burns, Oates and Washbourne, 1945).

White, W. D., ed.

The Preaching of John Henry Newman (Philadelphia: Fortress Press, 1969).

INDEX